A
SELZNICK INTERNATIONAL
PICTURE

SELZNICK INTERNATIONAL

in association with

METRO - GOLDWYN - MAYER

has the honor to present its

TECHNICOLOR

production of

MARGARET MITCHELL'S

STORY OF THE OLD SOUTH

A CELEBRATION OF

GONE WITH THE WIND

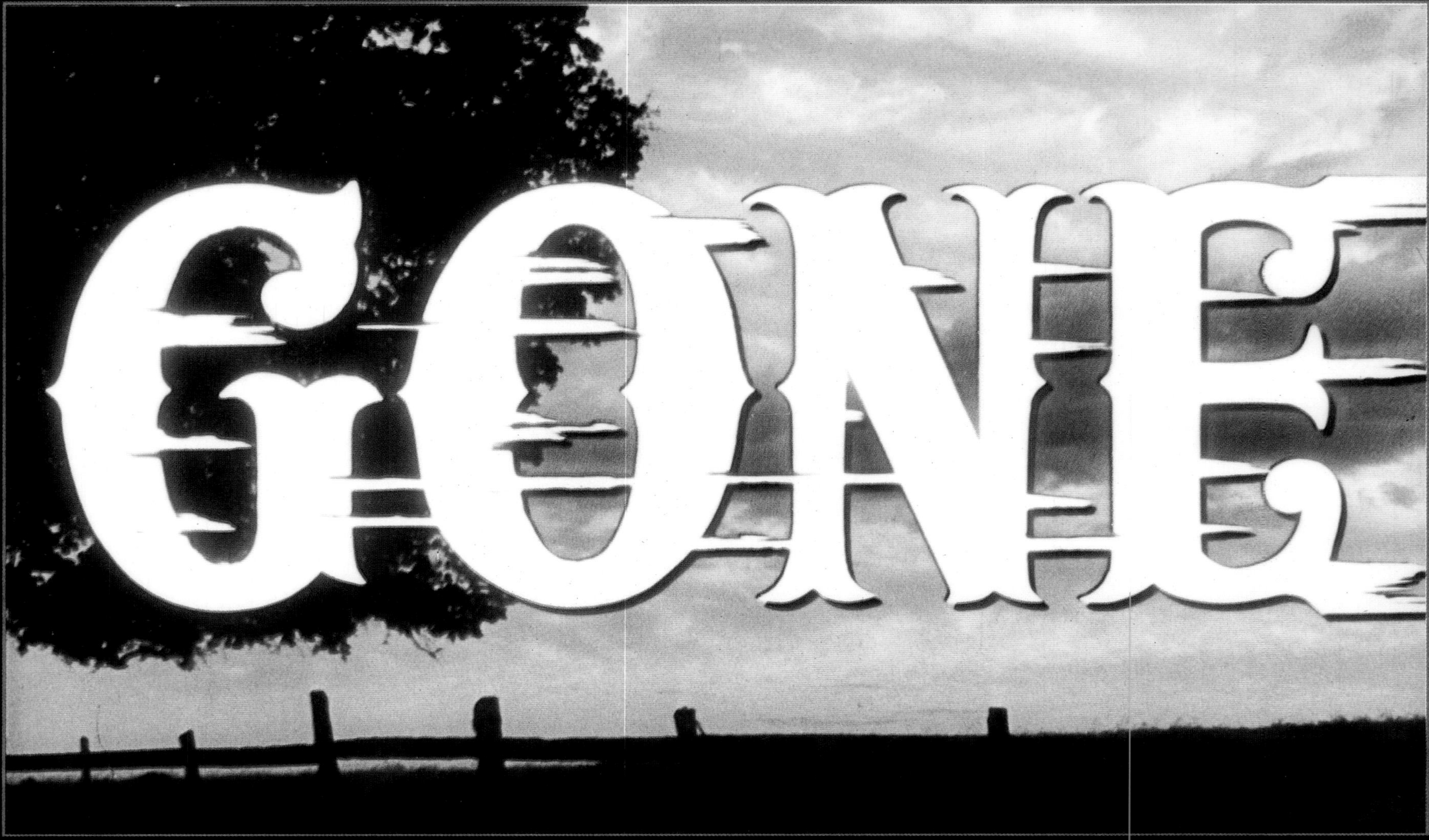
GONE

WITH

GONE WITH THE WIND

THE

This edition first published in 1990 by Gallery Books, an imprint of
W. H. Smith Publishers, Inc.,
112 Madison Avenue, New York 10016

Gallery Books are available for bulk purchase for sales promotions
and premium use. For details write or telephone the Manager
of Special Sales, W. H. Smith Publishers Inc., 112 Madison
Avenue, New York, New York 10016
(212) 532-6600

ISBN 0-8317-3913-4

DESIGNED BY JULIE AND STEVE RIDGEWAY ASSISTED BY DOLORES McCORMACK
MANAGING EDITOR PIPPA RUBINSTEIN
TYPESET BY BOOKWORM TYPESETTING, MANCHESTER

Printed and bound in Spain by

WIND

CONTENTS

Starring
CLARK GABLE
as
Rhett Butler

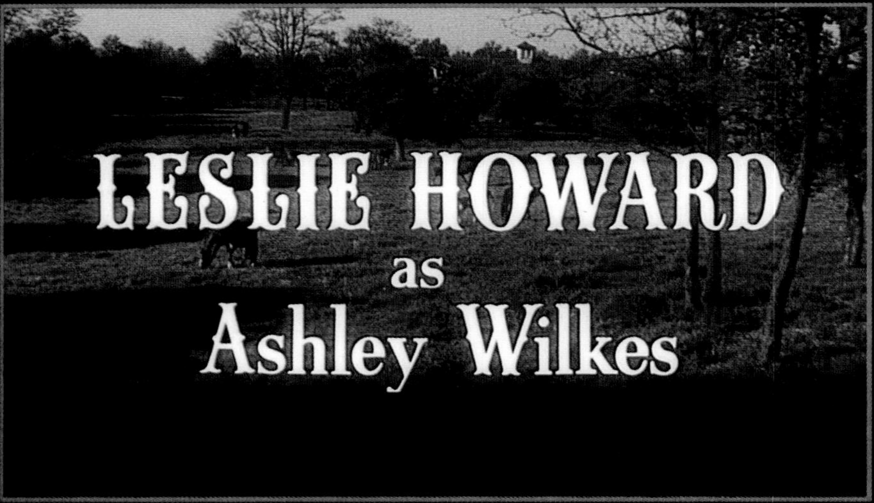

LESLIE HOWARD
as
Ashley Wilkes

OLIVIA de HAVILLAND
as
Melanie Hamilton

Musical Score
by
MAX STEINER

Screen Play
by
SIDNEY HOWARD

VIVIEN LEIGH
as
Scarlett O'Hara

This production designed by
WILLIAM CAMERON MENZIES

Special Photographic Effects
JACK COSGROVE

Photographed by . . . ERNEST HALLER, A.S.C.
Technicolor Associates:
RAY RENNAHAN, A.S.C.   WILFRID M. CLINE, A.S.C.
Art Direction by . . . . . . LYLE WHEELER
Interiors by . . . . . . JOSEPH B. PLATT
Interior Decoration by . . EDWARD G. BOYLE
Costumes designed by   WALTER PLUNKETT

Supervising Film Editor . . . . HAL C. KERN

Associate Film Editor . . . JAMES E. NEWCOM
Scenario Assistant . . . . BARBARA KEON
Production Manager . . RAYMOND A. KLUNE
Assistant Director . . . . ERIC G. STACEY
Recorder . . . . FRANK MAHER
Technicolor Co. Supervision. NATALIE KALMUS
Assistant Musical Director . . LOU FORBES

Historian . . . . WILBUR G. KURTZ

Directed
by
VICTOR FLEMING

Produced by
DAVID O. SELZNICK

AT TARA
The O'Hara Plantation in Georgia.

Gerald O'Hara	THOMAS MITCHELL
Ellen, *his wife*	BARBARA O'NEILL

Their Daughters:

Scarlett	VIVIEN LEIGH
Suellen	EVELYN KEYES
Carreen	ANN RUTHERFORD

Scarlett's beaux:

Brent Tarleton	GEORGE REEVES
Stuart Tarleton	FRED CRANE

The house servants:

Mammy	HATTIE McDANIEL
Pork	OSCAR POLK
Prissy	BUTTERFLY McQUEEN

In the fields

Jonas Wilkerson, *the overseer* .	VICTOR JORY
Big Sam, *the foreman* . .	EVERETT BROWN

AT TWELVE OAKS
The nearby Wilkes Plantation

John Wilkes	HOWARD HICKMAN
India, *his daughter* . .	ALICIA RHETT
Ashley, *his son* . .	LESLIE HOWARD
Melanie Hamilton, *their cousin* .	OLIVIA de HAVILLAND
Charles Hamilton, *her brother* .	RAND BROOKS
Frank Kennedy, *a guest* .	CARROLL NYE

and a visitor from Charleston

Rhett Butler	CLARK GABLE

IN ATLANTA

Aunt "Pittypat" Hamilton .	LAURA HOPE CREWS
Uncle Peter, *her coachman* .	EDDIE ANDERSON
Dr. Meade	HARRY DAVENPORT
Mrs. Meade	LEONA ROBERTS
Mrs. Merriwether . . .	JANE DARWELL
Belle Watling	ONA MUNSON

F O R E W O R D

Gone With the Wind is the definitive Hollywood picture. Released by Metro-Goldwyn-Mayer on 15 December 1939 at Loew's Grand Theater in Atlanta, Georgia, it continues to exert a peculiar fascination—as a love story, as a historical melodrama and as a popular myth. As a novel, as a movie continually re-released to cinemas, as a video, and even as a film soundtrack, there has always been and always will be an audience for it.

It is definitive because of the circumstances of its production and promotion rather than its merits as a work of art. It is definitive because of its enormous popularity and because it is a summation of Hollywood thinking and craftmanship at the time. *Gone With the Wind* marked the end of an era for Hollywood and, indeed, for America as well. Perhaps only *The Wizard of Oz*, released a few months earlier, and *Casablanca*, released in 1942, come close to matching it, for like *Gone With the Wind*, they exist as glorious monuments to a studio system that could withstand many changes of key personnel and a problematic script and still emerge in triumph. *Gone With the Wind* was born out of chaos, madness and a degree of luck.

Several hundred people contributed to the production of the film, including four directors, three lighting cameramen, perhaps a dozen screenwriters, numerous designers, art directors, editors, costume designers, special effects technicians, composers and publicists. Yet *Gone With the Wind* is really a monument to one man—its producer David O. Selznick.

At Selznick's funeral in 1965 Katharine Hepburn, just one of many actresses who might have played Scarlett O'Hara, chose to recite Kipling's poem 'If . . .' to summon up the arrogant, mad genius they were burying in Forest Lawn cemetery. Selznick would have relished the words,

> *If you can keep your head when all about you,*
> *Are losing theirs and blaming it on you,*

for they make an ideal epitaph to the man who created *Gone With the Wind*. Selznick kept his head and his independence and drove the film on to completion.

He would also have appreciated Kipling's thought, in the same poem, that triumph and disaster were both imposters. Selznick loved movies but he knew they were also a sham, a big show. In 1959, when the set of Tara was being dismantled and sent to Atlanta, Selznick said, 'Tara had no rooms inside. It was just a façade. Once photographed, life here is ended. It is almost symbolic of Hollywood.'

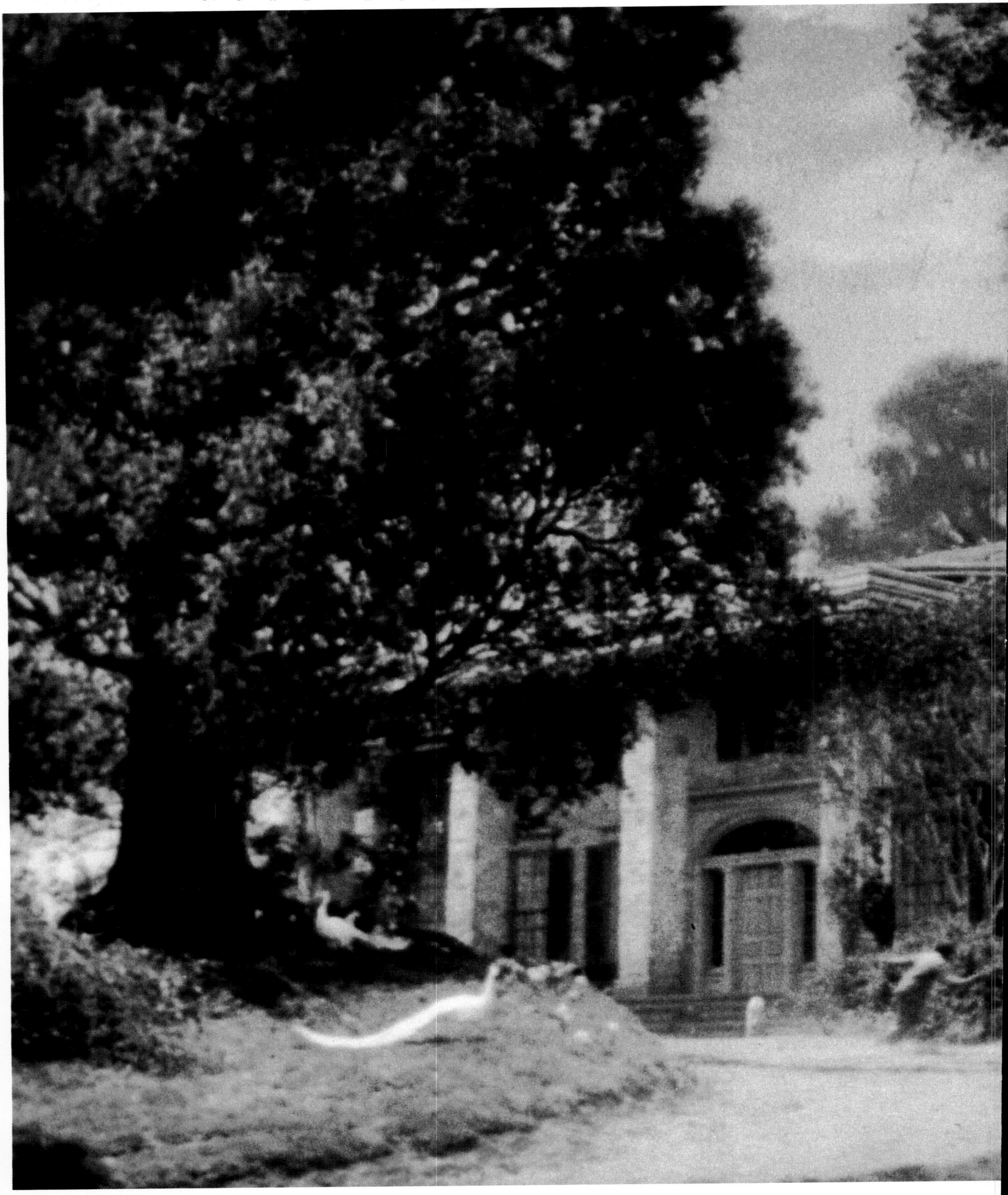

T H E   M A R S H E S   O F

A T L A N T A

In the beginning was the word; in fact, nearly half a million of them, written by Margaret Mitchell and published by Macmillan on 30 June 1936. She was born in Atlanta on 8 November 1900, the daughter of Eugene Muse and Maybelle (Stephens) Mitchell. They were a reasonably affluent family; young Margaret's paternal grandfather owned cotton plantations on the outskirts of the small town that was years away from becoming a city. She was educated at public schools in Atlanta and then attended Smith College in Northampton, Massachusetts. Her hopes for a career in medicine were dashed when her mother died during a flu epidemic in 1919, obliging Mitchell to return to Atlanta to run the house and look after her father and brother.

Towards the end of 1922 she was hired as a reporter for the *Atlanta Journal* for which she wrote features about the history of Atlanta based on her own research and interviews with senior citizens. Throughout her childhood her father regaled her with stories of Atlanta, the Old South and the Civil War. So vivid were her father's informal history lessons, that Mitchell thought the stories had occurred during her infancy rather than forty of fifty years previously. 'I was about ten years old before I learned the war hadn't ended shortly before I was born,' she wrote.

Margaret Mitchell of Atlanta

The empty-headed Tarleton twins, hoping to monopolize Scarlett's time at the forthcoming barbecue at the Wilkes' home, give Scarlett the news of Ashley Wilkes's engagement to his cousin Melanie.

In September of that year she married Berrien Kinnard Upshaw, a childhood sweetheart. Both were headstrong characters and the marriage lasted only three months. On Independence Day 1925 Mitchell married John Robert Marsh who had been Upshaw's best man. Marsh was an advertising executive for the Georgia Power Company, having previously been an English teacher and journalist. The couple moved into an apartment which an *Atlanta Journal* reporter described as 'physically dark but intellectually bright'.

Margaret Mitchell was a fragile woman, only 4 feet 11 inches tall, though

what she lacked in height she made up in character. A childhood riding accident, when she injured an ankle, left her physically vulnerable; she suffered from arthritis as well as recurrent bouts of severe eye-strain and other ailments. In 1926 she twisted her weak ankle and was forced to hobble around on crutches and remain indoors. She believed she would never walk unassisted again. It was her husband who urged her to write and so, as much to please him as to distract her thoughts from her physical disabilities, she embarked on a novel about Atlanta during the American Civil War.

Although Mitchell was always at pains to deny any direct parallels between herself and her heroine, Scarlett O'Hara, it is clear that she put more than just her accumulated historical knowledge into the sprawling plot. Mitchell was a very gregarious and headstrong person and Scarlett is nothing if not that. Of her marriages, people would say she had switched from Rhett Butler to Ashley Wilkes and that her disastrous and impetuous first marriage was similar to Scarlett's. The death of Mitchell's mother is directly echoed in the novel when Scarlett's mother dies during a typhoid epidemic. Even an incident in 1917, when Mitchell helped care for the injured during a major fire in Atlanta, is woven into the plot. And there is also the tone of the novel, written with a kind of innocent, childlike wonder about a bygone age, uncluttered by historical or political insights, so that it reads very much as Mitchell first heard it, as a child on her daddy's knee.

Deeply upset and jealous at the news of Ashley's engagement, Scarlett runs to greet her father. He tells her that one day Tara will be hers, though Scarlett is interested in beaux, not land.

Overleaf: 'Do you mean to tell me, Katie Scarlett O'Hara, that Tara, that land doesn't mean anything to you? Why, land is the only thing in the world worth working for, worth fighting for, worth dying for, because it's the only thing that lasts. It will come to you, this love of the land.'

In many ways, *Gone With the Wind* is the quintessential amateur novel, a private epic of gargantuan length commonly associated with women writers who, in most cases, consign them to the top shelf of the wardrobe. Apart from her features for the *Atlanta Journal*, Mitchell had published nothing. Her short stories were not submitted for publication and a novel about the Jazz Age was abandoned because she grew bored with the era and its obligatory sets of characters. Yet the vivacious, independently-minded Scarlett O'Hara is a character formed as much by the Jazz Age as by heroines from classical fiction, notably Becky Sharp in Thackeray's *Vanity Fair*, Charlotte Brontë's *Jane Eyre* and Natasha in Tolstoy's *War and Peace*. Scarlett's relationships with men, her liberated sexuality and, most of all, her resilience in the face of extreme adversity was essentially a 1920s conception that struck an immediate chord with American women who were achieving greater sexual equality and political expression.

Margaret Mitchell launched herself into the novel without any real preparation. 'I did not think about *Gone With the Wind* for years before it was written,' she said. 'A day came when I thought to myself, "Oh, my God, now I've got to write, and what is it going to be about?" and that day I started *Gone With the Wind*. I did not have to bother about my background, for it had been with me all my life. The plot, characters, etc., had not been with me. That day I thought I would write a story of a girl who was somewhat like Atlanta—part of the Old South, part of the New South;

how she rose with Atlanta and fell with it, and how she rose again. What Atlanta did to her; what she did to Atlanta—and the man who was more than a match for her. It didn't take me any time to get into my plot and characters. They were there and I took them and set them against the background which I knew as well as I did my own background.'

The plot follows the conventions of a national epic with characters swept along by the tide of history. The difference, perhaps, between Mitchell's epic and Tolstoy's *War and Peace* (casting aside matters of mere artistic achievement) is that the war in *Gone With the Wind* is often presented as little more than an obstacle to Scarlett's romantic ambitions, while Napoleon's invasion of Russia in *War and Peace* is rather more than an emotional set-back for Natasha. To be sure, characters in *Gone With the Wind* are always talking about the end of the world, as indeed do Tolstoy's characters, yet can we view that world's demise as tragic? Mitchell's heroes and heroines, after all, are prominent members of a society which owed its prosperity to slavery. Racial issues between blacks and whites hardly intruded into Mitchell's world; the only form of enslavement which interested her was between white men and white women.

The writing of *Gone With the Wind* took ten years. Mitchell said that had it not been for her arthritis, which crippled her hands, as well as attending to family and friends, she could have completed it in a year. After four years she had written

Mammy and Prissy squeeze Scarlett into her dress for the barbecue at Twelve Oaks.

The O'Haras arrive for the barbecue and Scarlett's eyes immediately search the mansion for a sight of her beloved Ashley.

about two-thirds of the story and kept the manuscript in manilla envelopes. In 1930 she moved house and her arthritis abated, enabling her to return to the social whirl. *Gone With the Wind* was put on the back-burner. Only the urging of her husband made her write in occasional bursts and in 1934 a car accident immobilized her once again.

Mitchell's interest in the novel had all but vanished and it might have lain unread and unfinished in her closet had it not been for a visit from an acquaintance, Harold Latham, in 1935. Latham worked for the publishing house of Macmillan in New York and had learned about Mitchell's novel from their mutual friend Lois Cole, an associate editor at Macmillan. Latham asked to see the manuscript and only at the insistence of her husband did Mitchell deliver a mountain of manilla envelopes to Latham's hotel. On the train to New York Latham read the manuscript, much of which was yellowed and smothered in corrections, instinctively smelt a blockbuster and offered to publish it. Mitchell had only to complete it and decide on a title. She was also persuaded to change the name of her heroine, from Pansy to Scarlett O'Hara.

There were several possible titles: 'Tomorrow Is Another Day', 'Bugles Sang True', 'Not in Our Stars' and 'Tote the Weary Load' were all considered and rejected. Mitchell finally, and in desperation, chose 'Gone With the Wind,' discovering the phrase in the second verse of a poem by Ernest Dowson called

'Cynara' which was published in 1891. The phrase had appeared rather more dramatically in a James Clarence Mangan poem of 1859, a fact unknown to Mitchell until it was pointed out to her, though it is assumed that this is where Dowson found the phrase himself. Within six months of Latham and Macmillan making their offer, Mitchell had decided on a title, edited the text and completed the missing sections. *Gone With the Wind* was finally ready for the printers. Publication date was announced for May 1936.

Macmillan believed the book to be something special, if only because it ran to 1037 pages, weighed two and a half pounds and would have a cover price of $3, which was 50 cents more than the usual novel. The print run was set at 10,000 copies. Macmillan's editors and publicity departments went to work and within weeks *Gone With the Wind* had become a publishing phenomenon, equalled only in recent years by Mario Puzo's *The Godfather*. When Mitchell's novel was selected by the influential Book-of-the-Month Club, a further printing of 30,000 copies became necessary. This not only obliged Macmillan to delay publication until 30 June, it enabled them to provide reviewers with finished copies of the book rather than galleys. It was also customary for publishers to send out new novels to the story editors of all the Hollywood studios. The asking price for the screen rights was $100,000, an unheard of sum for a first novel by an unknown writer, but a figure shrewdly calculated to intrigue Hollywood where money has

Ashley greets Scarlett and introduces her to Melanie, hoping they will become the closest of friends.

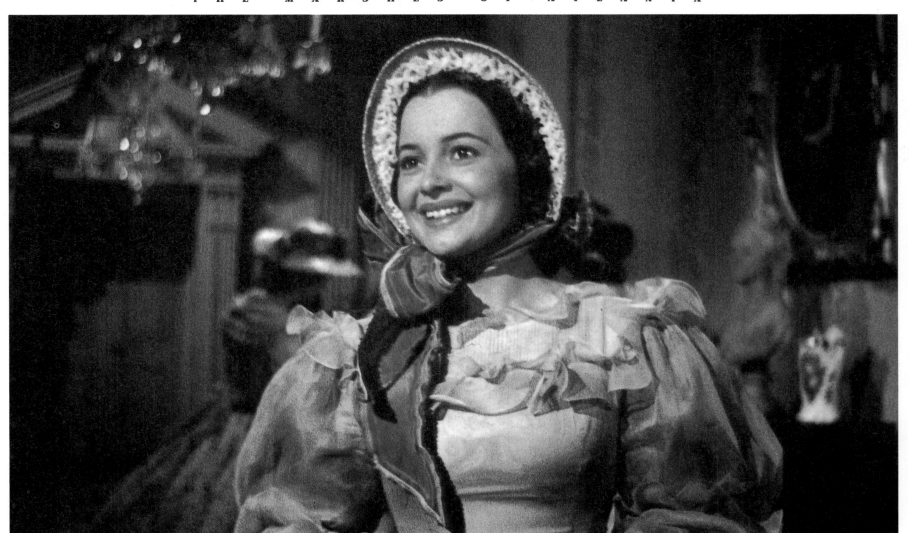

always been equated with quality.

Gone With the Wind became an instant best seller all over the world and won a Pulitzer Prize for fiction, earning its astonished author more than half a million dollars within a year of publication. However, Mitchell was quite unable to cope with the demands of celebrity and very quickly refused to give interviews or be photographed. She retreated into domestic anonymity, becoming plain Mrs Peggy Marsh of Atlanta, and toyed with the idea of writing a novel about sudden fame. But *Gone With the Wind* was to be her only published work.

Like the story and the characters she created, Margaret Mitchell became a myth. There were rumours about her marriage, her health, her reclusive lifestyle and the possibility that she might be quietly writing a sequel; there were even cases of women impersonating her in America and Latin America. The ironic truth is that Margaret Mitchell had created a monster that would not die.

Her longed-for escape was tragic. In 1945 her husband, John Marsh, suffered a heart attack. He never completely recovered and Mitchell nursed him with the kind of patient devotion one associates with Melanie Wilkes, Scarlett's rival and eventual friend in the novel. In the summer of 1949 she was out walking in Atlanta with her husband and was hit by a speeding taxi. She died five days later, having asked her husband to destroy the original manuscript of her one and only claim to fame. It was Peggy Marsh's final attempt to bury Margaret Mitchell.

Scarlett's eagle eye is caught by a stranger at the foot of the stairs. 'Who is that man?' 'That's Rhett Butler. He's from Charleston. He has the most terrible reputation.'

THE SELZNICKS

OF HOLLYWOOD

One day in May 1936 the chief executive of Metro-Goldwyn-Mayer, Louis B. Mayer, met with Irving G. Thalberg, MGM's principal producer and head of production, to consider a new project. Mayer preferred not to read stories or scripts; instead, a story editor, Kate Corbaley, often read the scripts to him. On this day it was a synopsis of a new novel called *Gone With the Wind*.

The two men listened to the saga of Scarlett O'Hara until Thalberg grew impatient. 'Forget it, Louis,' he said, 'No Civil War picture ever made a nickel.' 'Well, that's it,' said Mayer, 'Irving knows what's right.' This exchange has entered the annals of Hollywood mythology. Mayer, one of the founding fathers of Hollywood and virtual ruler of its greatest studio, and Irving Thalberg, the boy wonder who

Louis B. Mayer (left) with Marion Davies, Norma Shearer and Irving Thalberg

supposedly carried the entire finances of pictures in his head and was to receive immortality as the model for F. Scott Fitzgerald's *The Last Tycoon*, rejected what would become the most profitable film in Hollywood's history. By a twist of fate *GWTW*, as it quickly became known, would be released by MGM, two years after Thalberg's death at the age of thirty-seven.

In turning down *GWTW*, Mayer and Thalberg merely gave early proof of screenwriter William Goldman's 1980s maxim that in Hollywood 'Nobody knows anything'. Mayer and Thalberg were the last moguls to accept the coming of sound in 1928, publicly dismissing *The Jazz Singer* as a passing fad, partly because they genuinely thought it was, partly because they were jealous of Warner Brothers' technical breakthrough, and partly because MGM's New York-based parent company, Loew's Incorporated, blanched at the prospect of spending many millions of dollars equipping their chain of cinemas. Loew's was an immensely profitable corporation and within two years of its formation in 1924 MGM had become the biggest and the richest studio in Hollywood. Its success was founded on its stars and on the opulence of its pictures: Mayer and Thalberg were the ultimate purveyors of the 'American Dream'. They knew what had worked in the

past and safely assumed that it might do so again. Hollywood has generally been imitative rather than innovative; like the legal profession, it is based very largely on precedents. *GWTW* was hardly an innovative project; it was merely ambitious and expensive.

There is a peculiar irony to Thalberg's claim that Civil War pictures never made a nickel because it was just such a picture that made Mayer's fortune twenty years earlier. This was D. W. Griffith's *The Birth of a Nation*, arguably the most important film of Hollywood's silent era. Like *Gone With the Wind*, it is a love story, but the plot has a much more assertive and controversial political background for the lovers (two brothers and two sisters) are separated by North and South. The war forces a kind of reconciliation between the lovers, if not between the races: Blacks in Griffith's film are portrayed in decidedly racist tones, while the Ku Klux Klan emerge as the heroes.

Prior to *The Birth of a Nation* the American cinema was regarded by the intelligentsia and the middle and upper classes as a cheap entertainment patronized mainly by the immigrant working classes in sleazy nickelodeons. Griffith changed all that. The unprecedented scale of *The Birth of a Nation*—its sprawling narrative, elaborate battle sequences, its two-and-a-half hour running time and its celebration of white supremacy—attracted vast attention. The political controversy, which resulted in several riots and unsuccessful attempts by

Watched by the jealous Scarlett, Ashley and Melanie stroll through the sun-drenched, verdant grounds of Twelve Oaks. Ashley is in a melancholy mood, convinced that war is inevitable and that their lives will be ruined. But Melanie says, 'We don't have to be afraid for us. No war can come into our world, Ashley. Whatever comes, I'll love you, just as I do now, until I die.'

the newly-founded National Association for the Advancement of Colored People (NAACP) to have the film banned, meant that for the first time the cinema was taken seriously—as a social and political force, as an industry and as an art.

In 1915 Louis B. Mayer was chairman of a small production company called Metro. A former scrap metal merchant, Mayer had become a local exhibitor and then a distributor. He realized that he had to become a producer as well to create a profitable business. *The Birth of a Nation* was his big break. As he later told the star of the film, Lillian Gish, 'I was running a group of theatres in Haverhill, Massachusetts, where I'd started out with a nickelodeon. When *The Birth of a Nation* came along, I pawned everything I owned—my house, my insurance, even my wife's wedding ring—just to get the New England states' rights. Since then, everything's been very pleasant. If it hadn't been for D. W. Griffith, *The Birth*, and you, I'd still be in Haverhill.'

Although Mayer rather over-dramatizes his acquisition of Griffith's epic—he and his partners paid $50,000—it has been estimated that from profits of $600,000 Mayer's personal share would have been $150,000, enabling him to move to California and play his own part in the creation of Hollywood. So when, some twenty years later, Irving Thalberg said, 'Forget it, Louis. No Civil War picture ever made a nickel,' he was forgetting what the most successful film in history had been up to that point. Is it possible that the irony was lost on Louis?

Mayer and Thalberg were not alone in their rejection of *GWTW*. David O. Selznick turned it down as well. He was a man who liked to commit everything to paper, a personal trait often associated with paranoids but here the habit of a man fully aware of the social importance of what he was doing as much as his own grandeur. Memos allowed Selznick to argue with himself; he was a great ditherer because, for a perfectionist, there is no such thing as perfection.

The records show that on 20 May 1936 he was viewing a rough-cut of his production *The Garden of Allah* when his story editor in New York, Kay Brown, cabled an excited message: 'Have just airmailed detailed synopsis of *Gone With the Wind* by Margaret Mitchell, also copy of book. This is an absolutely magnificent story, a great literary property and we must have it. The book is 1000 pages long and I have only gotten through half of it. It is one of the most lush things I ever read. I am absolutely off my nut about this book. I beg, urge, coax and plead with you to read it at once. I know that after you do you will drop everything and buy it.'

Selznick read the synopsis and did not buy it. On 25 May he cabled Kay Brown, sharing some of her enthusiasm for the story but worrying about its price and about casting since he had no suitable stars under contract for the leading roles. He wanted to wait to see how the book was received and, like Thalberg, he believed that Civil War pictures were unpopular. (Paramount had released *So Red the Rose* in 1935 to empty houses.) 'Most sorry to have to say no in face of your enthusiasm for this story,' Selznick concluded. In her autobiography, his then wife Irene recalled, 'The company was less than a year old when David asked me if I wanted to see a movie of a Civil War story. Of course I didn't. *He* didn't. No one did, not conceivably. It was a first novel, carrying a stiff price and a terrible title. All that and the Civil War besides.'

However, the next day Selznick had a slight change of heart. He cabled Brown and suggested she contact the director Merian C. Cooper and Jock Whitney, chairman of the board of Selznick International Pictures (and a future US ambassador to Britain), to consider the project as a 'possible colour picture, especially if they can sell the very colourful man's role to Gary Cooper. Were I with MGM, I believe I would buy it now for some such combination as Gable and Joan Crawford.'

Many more exchanges of cables were to follow, with Selznick speculating about casting and worrying about the cost of the screen rights and production costs. At the same time, other studios were beginning to show interest, principally

David O. Selznick of Hollywood

While the women and children sleep off their lunch upstairs, Scarlett eavesdrops on a meeting between the men. The talk is of war and Rhett infuriates the others by his pragmatism: 'All we've got is cotton and slaves and …arrogance.'
Overleaf: After the meeting, Scarlett meets Ashley in the library and declares her love for him. But it is to no avail: 'Melanie's like me, Scarlett. She's part of my blood and we understand each other. You have all the passion for life that I lack, but that kind of love of life isn't enough to make a marriage between two people as different as we are.'

because, like Kay Brown, women adored the novel. Katharine Hepburn tried to persuade the president of RKO, Pandro Berman, to buy it for her, and Bette Davis was doing the same with Jack Warner. Meanwhile, weeks from publication, Macmillan's asking price was coming down. An offer of $45,000 was on the table from RKO. Realizing that *GWTW* might quickly slip from her grasp, Kay Brown found an ally in Jock Whitney who advised Selznick that he would buy the book for Pioneer Pictures, Whitney's other film company. This ploy had the desired effect as Selznick immediately authorized an offer of $50,000 which Mitchell, having been advised that she could expect no more, accepted.

The news of the sale of *GWTW* to Selznick prompted a sudden rush of would-be gazumpers. RKO, still under pressure from Katharine Hepburn, offered $55,000 but Mitchell, who was in New York, turned them down, having already committed herself. On 30 July 1936 she met with Kay Brown to draw up the contract, warning the representatives of Selznick International that they would have great problems if they tried to reduce the plot of her novel. 'It had taken me ten years to weave it as tight as a silk pocket handkerchief,' she said.

The contract gave Selznick 'exclusive, complete and entire motion picture and broadcasting rights, including television [this in 1936], in the property known as *Gone With the Wind....* The owner shall not be responsible for any additions, adaptations, substitutions or other changes the purchaser may make, or for any

Hysterical, Scarlett slaps Ashley and after he leaves the room she tosses a porcelain vase across the room. 'Has the war started?' asks a surprised Rhett who has been hiding behind a settee. Attracted by Scarlett's anger he says, 'I hope to see more of you when you are free of the spell of the elegant Mr Wilkes. He doesn't strike me as half-good enough for your, what was it...your passion for living?'

words or any delineation or interpretation of character different than that contained in the property.'

Selznick now had to read the mighty tome which had cost him $50,000. He took it with him on holiday to Honolulu, 'as did half the passengers on the boat', recalled Irene Selznick. The synopsis did not prepare him for the extraordinary detail and the rich characterizations that Mitchell had created. He wondered who would star in it, write it and direct it. He wondered how he could possibly adapt a novel that seemingly everyone in United States had read and loved so much that even the smallest change would infuriate them. Most of all he wondered how much it would cost, for Selznick, though already one of Hollywood's major movie producers, did not have the resources of a major studio like MGM. He was an independent by nature and by design.

David O. Selznick was the son of Lewis J. Selznick, one of the American cinema's pioneer producers. Selznick senior was born Lewis Zeleznik on 2 May 1870 in Kiev, Russia. He had seventeen brothers and sisters, lived in conditions of some poverty and grew up in the perpetual shadow of sometimes violent anti-Semitism. He somehow made his way to England and worked in a factory until he had saved enough money to leave for the United States as one of 'the huddled masses yearning to breathe free'. He settled in Pittsburgh in 1882 and got a job as a jeweller's apprentice. The appalling memory of years of poverty in

What began as a social gathering has turned into a call to arms. The men mount up and go to enlist in the Confederate Army. Scarlett receives a sudden proposal of marriage from Melanie's brother, the clumsy and stupid Charles Hamilton. Scarlett cares nothing for him but as she watches Ashley kiss Melanie goodbye, she accepts Charles's proposal on an impulse. Charles can hardly believe his ears.

Russia and the dream of the New World drove Selznick senior on and by 1894 he owned his own jewellery store, The Keystone, on Smithfield Street. This street has a claim to fame, not as the site of Selznick's store but as the site of the United States first nickelodeon which opened on Thanksgiving Eve 1905 with a showing of *The Great Train Robbery*. Selznick could claim he was there at the very beginning, if only as a paying customer.

Now married and with three sons—Myron, Howard and David—Lewis Selznick and family moved to New York in 1910, selling the jewellery business two years later. Like his contemporaries—Adolph Zukor, Louis B. Mayer, William Fox, Marcus Loew, Sam Goldwyn and Carl Laemmle—Selznick saw the potential of the 'flickers' which had become the immigrants' principal source of cheap entertainment. Within a few years his career as a pioneer movie mogul had taken off; he had his own studio and contract stars. His slogan was 'Selznick Pictures Make Happy Hours'. However, Selznick was not wholly committed to the movie business; unlike Zukor or Goldwyn, he had no passion for movies and saw them simply as a way of earning a decent living and maintaining his family in some style. He gave his sons lavish personal allowances, advising them to spend it all and stay broke.

Three things contributed to Selznick senior's undoing: he was addicted to gambling and ran up massive debts, he made some poor business and creative decisions, and his relations with the other moguls, such as Zukor and Fox, were far from harmonious. In 1923, unable to pay his creditors, he was declared bankrupt. An attempt to revive his fortunes in Florida real estate and then radio also failed. Lewis then attempted to make some capital out of MGM's screen adaptation of *Ben Hur* (1925) by buying the company which owned the stage rights. At the meeting, which was attended by David, the president of Loew's, Nick Schenck, managed to stop Selznick's scheme dead in its tracks. He did, however, promise to help David if the need ever arose. Lewis died in 1933, supported in the last years of his life by his two sons, Myron and David. The other son, Howard, who was said to suffer from a brain defect, faded from public view and from history.

Myron Selznick was born on 5 October 1898 and by the age of twenty-one had become head of production at his father's studio. When his father's business collapsed he tried to make a career as an independent producer but in 1928 he abandoned production and became one of Hollywood's most powerful talent agents.

David Selznick was born on 10 May 1902. Like his older brother, he too went into the family business and when it collapsed he hoped to make a career for himself as a writer. This came to nothing, so he then made two film documentaries—the first, a boxing story, and the second, an account of a beauty contest judged by matinée idol Rudolph Valentino, which earned Selznick $15,000. In 1926 he arrived in Hollywood and got himself a job in MGM's story department. When Mayer learned of this appointment he shouted, 'No Selznick will ever work at MGM!' His antipathy dated back to 1918 when he had formed a brief, unhappy partnership with Lewis J. Selznick, the memory of which still hurt.

Both Myron and David Selznick had an innate resentment, which they barely suppressed, of the Hollywood establishment. They blamed the studio moguls for their father's bankruptcy and for their sudden plummet from a life of luxury to one of more ordinary comforts. Myron determined to avenge his father by signing up stars and raising their asking price; in fact, he was the prototype of the agents who were to take over Hollywood in the 1960s and 1970s. Unlike his father, David Selznick's passion for movies was total; his entire career was dedicated to the business and to achieving total independence. His productions would redeem the family name.

When he learned that Mayer did not welcome him with open arms, Selznick appealed to Mayer's boss, Nick Schenck, reminding him of his promise at the *Ben Hur* meeting. Selznick's appointment was quickly confirmed. He acquitted himself well and his relations with Mayer improved. Selznick rose rapidly from menial script-reader to head of the script department to production supervisor of B-westerns which starred Tim McCoy. His ability to handle the production line of B-pictures, as well as his fertile yet usually practical imagination, made him rise still further until, in 1928, he was made assistant to the powerful producer Hunt Stromberg on MGM's first sound picture, *White Shadows of the South Seas*. Selznick disagreed with Stromberg over the kind of picture they were making and took his problems to Irving Thalberg. Since Thalberg himself had dictated to Stromberg what kind of picture it should be, Selznick had made a tactical error. Thalberg sided with Stromberg and Selznick was fired.

Scarlett is barely married when she learns that her husband has died of pneumonia. She feigns grief with her mother who suggests a visit to Atlanta where Scarlett can stay with Aunt Pittypat and Melanie. It is not an attractive idea until she realizes that Ashley might be there as well . . .
Overleaf: At the Atlanta Bazaar Scarlett and Melanie renew their acquaintance with Rhett, now celebrated as a heroic blockade-runner, and contribute their wedding rings to the cause. More money is raised when the men bid for their dancing partners and Scarlett, dressed in mourning but filled with life, outrages Atlanta society by accepting Rhett's bid for the Virginia reel. As they dance he says, 'Someday I want you to say the words to me that you said to Ashley Wilkes. I love you.'

Instead of finding himself out on the street, he became assistant to the legendary B. P. Schulberg, the head of production at Paramount Pictures. At the same time, Selznick was courting Irene Mayer, Louis B. Mayer's daughter. They married in April 1930 and spent part of their two-month honeymoon in Washington as the guests of President and Mrs Herbert Hoover. Even if Selznick's professional ambitions had yet to be realized, socially he had more than merely arrived.

Selznick's tenure at Paramount was brief and dramatic. Hollywood was enbroiled not only in the sound revolution but was hit as well by the stock market crash and the Depression. He finally resigned from Paramount in June 1931 after he refused to accept a cut in salary. Yet Selznick formed some interesting associations at Paramount and initiated, or suggested, some remarkable pictures, including Merian C. Cooper and Ernest B. Schoedsack's classic adventure drama *The Four Feathers* (1929). In February 1931 he expressed his admiration for Laurence Olivier as a possible star at Paramount, though the financial terms demanded by Olivier's agent—none other than brother Myron—put an end to it. Most importantly, as far as this story is concerned, Selznick became friendly with George Cukor, a stage director newly arrived from New York, and arranged Cukor's first Hollywood job as dialogue director on *All Quiet on the Western Front* (1930).

After being fired by MGM and having resigned on principle from Paramount,

Hushed and grim, the old men, women and children of Atlanta assemble to read the list of those fallen at the Battle of Gettysburg. To Scarlett and Melanie's relief, Ashley's name is not on the list.

Killed in action.
Injuries and capture
Killed in action.
Killed in action.
Killed in action.
Killed in action.
Captured.
Killed in action.
Killed in action.
Head wound, captu
Killed in action.

Selznick decided to strike out on his own as an independent producer. He found a partner in Lewis Milestone, the director of the acclaimed *All Quiet on the Western Front*, and sought financial backing from a major studio. At the time, the studios distributed their own pictures to their own chains of cinemas so Selznick had to become an independent subsidiary in order to guarantee the distribution of his films. But no one was prepared to back his venture, least of all his father-in-law who saw Selznick's venture as a possible first chink in the armour of the Hollywood establishment—a milieu where 'independent' was a four-letter word.

In New York it looked as if Selznick and Milestone might have found financial backing from Cornelius Vanderbilt Whitney. But Milestone then accepted an offer from United Artists, leaving Selznick without his star director. Also in New York was Merian C. Cooper, with whom Selznick had sparred at Paramount over the making of *The Four Feathers*. Nevertheless, the two became firm friends and during Selznick's efforts to establish himself as an independent, Cooper described a picture he wanted to make that had been turned down by every studio he approached. It was to be a fantasy story with a lot of complicated special effects. Its title was *King Kong*.

Cooper, a director of unusual influence and a talented manipulator of executives, devised a highly intricate scheme whereby Selznick would become head of production at a studio which would give the green light to the gorilla

Atlanta prayed while onward surged the triumphant Yankees. Heads were high, but hearts were heavy as the wounded and the refugees poured into unhappy Georgia. Scarlett has become a nurse and helps Dr Meade care for the wounded and the dying. But Scarlett's charitable spirit is not boundless; sickened by death and lice and mutilated men, she runs away from her duty.

picture. Thus, in October 1931, David Selznick was appointed vice-president of production at the ailing RKO Pictures on a weekly salary of $2500. Selznick's contract also enabled him to select a certain number of films which he would personally supervise. In effect, he was in an identical position to Irving Thalberg at MGM. The only drawback was that, like Thalberg, Selznick was answerable to a board of directors. Complete independence still eluded him.

Under Selznick's guidance RKO's fortunes and reputation were considerably enhanced. He sponsored the career of a young producer, Pandro Berman, who would eventually end up running the studio; he sponsored the career of George Cukor who directed *What Price Hollywood?* (1932)—a film Selznick would remould in 1937 as *A Star Is Born*—as well as *A Bill of Divorcement* (1932) with Katharine Hepburn; and he did indeed approve the production of *King Kong* (1933), which became one of the first great masterpieces of the talkie era. But by the time *King Kong* was released Selznick's career had taken another significant step forward. On 16 February 1933 he found himself at Metro-Goldwyn-Mayer again, this time as an executive producer answerable only to Louis B. Mayer. The story of the appointment in the trade paper the *Hollywood Reporter* was headlined, 'The Son-in-Law Also Rises'.

Thalberg had suffered a heart attack and was convalescing with his wife, Norma Shearer, in the South of France. Mayer hired his son-in-law not as an eventual replacement for Thalberg but simply to help him run the studio and originate and produce the prestige pictures that had been Thalberg's speciality.

Selznick and Thalberg were close personal friends and shared a similar attitude to their work; they both believed the producer was the principal author of a picture. They respected directors but regarded them as dispensable; writers were simply machines. Stars, on the other hand, demanded reverence and patience for they were the reason why audiences went to the movies. Selznick and Thalberg also shared a weakness for the weighty novel and the in-built prestige it brought them. However, the differences between the two men were also considerable: Thalberg was quiet, unassuming, an intellectual with the demeanour of a banker or civil servant. Selznick, from now on, would grow into an obsessive who thrived on personal publicity. But the greatest difference between Thalberg and Selznick was that Thalberg instinctively avoided risk—he was a company man who played safe. Selznick had inherited his father's passion for gambling and loved a risk.

Audiences expected lavishness from MGM and they got it. Selznick had brought Cukor to MGM and together they made their studio début with *Dinner at Eight* (1933), a sparkling all-star Broadway adaptation that was so much better than Thalberg's equivalent, the well-upholstered but lumpen *Grand Hotel* (1931). *Manhattan Melodrama* (1934) with Gable, was an enormous money-spinner, and *Reckless* (1935) with Jean Harlow, marked Selznick's first association with Victor Fleming, one of the studio's highest paid directors. But Selznick's most important films at MGM were three ambitious and lavish literary adaptations: Dickens' *David Copperfield* (1934) directed by Cukor, and *A Tale of Two Cities* (1935), and Tolstoy's *Anna Karenina* (1935).

By the time the last of these films, *A Tale of Two Cities*, was in production, Thalberg had returned to MGM and was fully installed as an executive producer. Selznick, realising that a triumvirate of himself, Thalberg and Mayer was unworkable, announced his resignation on 27 June 1935. A shower of offers from other studios arrived but he determined to form his own company.

Selznick's first investor, much to his amazement and delight, was Irving Thalberg who offered $200,000 in Norma Shearer's name. With a further $200,000 from his brother Myron, Selznick went to New York to look for the bulk of his capital. Through Merian C. Cooper, who by now had become production chief at RKO, Selznick was introduced to John ('Jock') Hay Whitney, an East Coast financier and millionaire who had little or no show business connections and was not Jewish. Whitney invested $2.4 million and became chairman of the board. An additional $300,000 of investment capital came from New York bankers and John Hertz, who ran a fleet of taxicabs which would eventually become the world's biggest car rental agency.

In Hollywood Selznick bought the old Thomas Ince studio which was just down the road from MGM and looked like a lavish southern plantation mansion. The first employee to sign on was director George Cukor. Kay Brown was hired to run the New York office, alerting Selznick to potential story material. A distribution deal was concluded with United Artists. Selznick International was in business.

At the formation of his company, Selznick told reporters, 'The day of mass production has ended. It has become, in the making of good pictures, so essential for a producer to collaborate on every inch of script, to be available for every

Overleaf: Outside there is panic as Sherman's shells hit Atlanta. Columns of soldiers and fleeing citizens choke the streets and only Rhett saves Scarlett from being trampled underfoot. He suggests they escape together to Mexico, London or Paris. 'I hate and despise you Rhett Butler, and I'll hate and despise you till I die.' 'Oh no, not that long,' smiles Rhett. Scarlett is deposited safely just as Aunt Pittypat is leaving the city. Scarlett wants to go too, home to Tara to take care of her mother who is ill, but Dr Meade insists she stays to look after Melanie who is expecting Ashley's child.

conference and go over all the details of production that is physically impossible for him to give his best efforts to more than a limited number of pictures. My object as a producer has always been to make the finer things, and to leave the trash to the other fellows. I firmly believe that the future of pictures lies in producing stories of high calibre.'

Selznick was as good as his word: he wrote memos, pestered directors on the set, rewrote scripts, masterminded publicity campaigns and strove for the finer things. *A Star Is Born* (1937) was certainly that, a lavish Technicolor evocation of Hollywood and a star's rise and fall. But *Little Lord Fauntleroy* (1936) and *The Garden of Allah* (1936) had more flummery than the finery to which Selznick aspired.

So now, in the summer of 1936, David O. Selznick had bought Margaret Mitchell's *Gone With the Wind*. Its challenge both exhilarated and frightened him. He could not be other than inspired by a novel which, in so many ways, resembled himself: deeply romantic, verbose, a hymn to human survival—he might have cried into his dictaphone, 'As God is my witness, I'll never be a studio employee again!' Selznick was his own man now; there was no one to answer to, no one to appease, no need to compromise. He could look back on several major successes that were his own work and look forward to an epic that would make his father proud, that would astonish Hollywood and affirm his place in its pantheon.

THE MAN WHO WOULD

BE KING

Right from the outset Margaret Mitchell made it clear she wanted nothing to do with Hollywood or the production of the picture. After all, making movies was Selznick's job, not hers.

Nevertheless, she was hounded by her readers and the press who implored her not to allow Hollywood to change so much as a word. Most of all, like Selznick, she was inundated with letters regarding the casting. In a letter to Kay Brown, Mitchell said, 'I suppose you know that casting this picture is the favourite drawing-room game these days and every newspaper has been after me to say just who I want to play the parts. It has been difficult but so far I have kept my mouth shut. I wish to goodness you all would announce the cast and relieve me of this burden!' Apart from appearing to endorse Katharine Hepburn's candidacy for the role of Scarlett O'Hara (a slip which brought about a rapid apology), the most Mitchell had said was that for the part of Rhett Butler she would be happy with Groucho Marx or Donald Duck.

Melanie is in labour, preventing their evacuation from the city. Scarlett goes in search of Dr Meade and has to walk across the station yard which has become the resting place for hundreds of wounded and dying soldiers.

Director, George Cukor

In the end, Mitchell wrote to Louella Parsons, whose syndicated movie column was devoured by millions of readers who took its rumours and hearsay as gospel. 'I am appealing as a harassed and weary author,' she wrote, 'sadly in need of a rest and unable to get it because of the mail and telegrams that flood in on me due to rumours which seem to be circulating all over the country.' In her column of 23 October 1936 Parsons had claimed that Mitchell was going blind, that doctors had forbidden her to travel to California and that no casting could be finalized without her approval. In her letter Mitchell politely refuted these allegations and Parsons duly complied with another column. The mail and the telegrams abated and Mitchell was able to rest and let Selznick get on with it.

Casting the picture was a national obsession which would become both Selznick's agony and his greatest publicity stunt. But before those dramatic, conclusive decisions were made he needed a director, a writer and a team of technicians. He also needed the money.

Selznick's first decision, made in Hawaii, was that George Cukor should direct the picture. In many ways Cukor was the inevitable choice. The two men knew each other well, enjoyed each other's company, and Cukor owed Selznick allegiance for having sponsored his career at Paramount, RKO and MGM. Cukor was also a gifted director of actresses. Thanks to his razor wit, highly cultured intelligence and homosexuality, actresses trusted, conspired with and confided in him. He was not a sexual threat but a close friend. Whoever played Scarlett O'Hara would have to carry the entire picture. She would need a man like Cukor to guide her along the path.

He was born in New York in 1899, a second-generation American whose grandparents had emigrated from Hungary. He originally intended to become a lawyer but soon turned towards the theatre, becoming one of Broadway's leading directors. When sound arrived Hollywood plundered Broadway for directors and dialogue coaches. Cukor soon found himself aboard a train for the West Coast.

Cukor specialized in directing Broadway adaptations and extracting great performances; he delighted in theatricality, mas-
querades and grand deceptions.

Screenwriter, Sidney Howard

He was not interested in big statements, like Frank Capra, and neither was he interested in big action sequences. He was an interior director for whom drama resulted from the intimate interplay of character. He was relatively slow and extremely fastidious.

Gone With the Wind had a narrative sweep beyond anything Cukor had attempted before, including *David Copperfield*, and would ultimately require speed more than art. Cukor wanted *GWTW* to combine his favoured drawing-room scenes with lavish reconstructions of Civil War battles which were hardly his forte. Selznick restrained him from going 'overboard on size and expensive production scenes of the Civil War, which I think should be shown mainly in terms of its effect on our principals. . . .'

Selznick now required a writer willing to tackle the 1037 pages of the original novel. His relationship with screenwriters was never less than fraught since he believed they should work closely with him and that every scene and every line of dialogue should be argued over until it was right. He needed his writer in Hollywood, in an adjoining office if possible, and available twenty-four hours a day. Sidney Howard could not agree to this.

Selznick chose Howard because he regarded him, along with Ben Hecht, as the best screenwriter who was not under contract to a Hollywood studio. Howard knew about dramatic structure and was capable of producing twenty-five pages of script a day. He had won a Pulitzer Prize for his play, *They Knew What They Wanted*, and had scripted *Arrowsmith* (1931) and *Dodsworth* (1936) for producer Sam Goldwyn and had received Academy Award nominations for both.

Born in 1891 in California, Howard lived on a 700-acre cattle ranch in Tyringham, Massachusetts—real Yankee territory. He was a close friend of Merian C. Cooper, having flown with him during World War I, so Selznick naturally enlisted Cooper's help in securing Howard's services. Howard accepted Selznick's offer but refused to leave his cows. He knew that writing was a solitary occupation and that Hollywood could never appreciate the fact. Like virtually all East Coast writers and intellectuals, he had contempt for Hollywood's production-line methods but welcomed the considerable financial rewards. The last thing he wanted was a crazy producer leaning over his shoulder and arguing about every comma. Selznick had no choice but to accept Howard's insistence that they should collaborate over a distance of 3000 miles.

Howard signed his contract in October and on 14 December 1936 Selznick received a fifty-page memo from him which laid out the basic structure and explained what he planned on deleting from the novel. He wanted to cut several of the O'Hara clan from the story as well as some other secondary characters. Howard also proposed several montage sequences to portray the progress of the war and suggested that Rhett Butler's blockade-running activities be shown rather than, as in the novel, simply taken on trust. It was not a treatment, nor was it a script; it was an intelligent and perceptive appraisal of a gripping, emotionally overwhelming, if discursive, novel.

Selznick read and re-read Howard's submission over Christmas and replied on 6 January 1937. He was pleased with Howard's outline but warned him against inventing new material or making minor changes. Howard could bring down the guillotine on complete characters and episodes, but what remained should not be tampered with. 'I am embarrassed to say this to you who have been so outstandingly successful in your adaptations, but I find myself a producer charged with re-creating the best-beloved book of our time, and I don't think any of us have tackled anything that is really comparable in the love that people have for it.'

It was all to do with preserving the 'chemicals' of a story, even if that meant respecting structural flaws. Selznick later told the film critic and biographer of MGM and Mayer, Bosley Crowther, 'If there are faults in construction it is better to keep them than try to change them around because no one can certainly pick out the chemicals which contribute to the making of a classic. And there is always the danger that by tampering, you may destroy the essential chemical.'

However, one of the chemicals in Mitchell's novel did alarm both Howard and Selznick. Howard wanted to eliminate all of Mitchell's references to the Ku Klux Klan: 'Because of the lynching problems we have on our hands these days,' he

wrote, 'I hate to indulge in anything which makes the lynching of a Negro in any sense sympathetic.' Selznick agreed; he did not want to invite the same sort of hostility that Griffith attracted with *The Birth of a Nation*.

Race relations were a major issue in the United States during the 1930s and lynchings in the South were common. At that time, novelists such as William Faulkner and Upton Sinclair were exploring racial issues with considerable force. In this sense, Mitchell's picture of the Old South, with its compliant, docile and childish Negroes, seemed a regression.

Selznick was made aware of this when the book was published; reviews from Black sections of the literary community were extremely hostile. One reviewer, L. D. Reddick, said, 'This book is written with a passionate sectional and racial bias. It is almost painfully weak in the handling of the larger social forces implicit in the materials.' In the coming months Selznick and Howard would take great care over this aspect of the screenplay, deleting the Ku Klux Klan but retaining the use of the word 'nigger'. When Black actors were tested they felt insulted and complained to the NAACP which immediately launched a campaign calling for a boycott of the picture by Black actors and, eventually, Black audiences.

Selznick's attitude was typical of the affluent middle classes: he wanted to bestow dignity upon the Negroes without allowing them to rise above their social station. Yet the Jew in Selznick pricked his conscience: 'I feel so keenly about what is happening to the Jews of the world that I cannot help but sympathize with the Negroes in their fears, however unjustified they may be, about material which they regard as insulting or damaging.' Selznick immediately courted leading Black writers and, once shooting had started, invited Black journalists on to the set. But it was a publicity campaign and not to be taken seriously. *GWTW* was a love story, not a documentary, and Selznick vetoed the suggestion that he hire an official Black adviser. He sent a memo to Jock Whitney: 'We're surrounded now on all sides by advisers [and] one more will only confuse us. Such a person would probably want to remove what comedy we have built around the Negroes, no matter how lovable we have made them.' Butterfly McQueen, who was to play the stupid maid Prissy, was appalled by the characterization. 'I hated that role,' she said in 1989, 'I thought the movie was going to show the progress Black people had made, but Prissy was lazy and stupid and backward.' Even by the standards of the 1930s, Selznick showed little genuine interest in anything beyond the story of Rhett and Scarlett. Everything else was just background.

Howard delivered the first draft of the screenplay in the summer of 1937. It ran to 400 pages which would have amounted to a six-hour picture. Selznick always had in the back of his mind a running time of two-and-a-half hours and a budget of around $2 million. Howard's script made him realize that *GWTW* could not possibly come that cheaply. It was a slightly reduced version of the novel which had some fine writing and a good sense of structure. But something had happened to the chemicals. Selznick was alarmed how Howard's style, his dislike of the grand emotional gesture, his preference for understatement, had doused some of the flames in the story. Perhaps the most graphic example of Howard's reticence was his deletion of the scene that closes Part One of the film (but in the novel occurs as Scarlett leaves the shattered Twelve Oaks and sets out for Tara) when Scarlett has her great speech of determination and survival: 'As God is my witness, I'll never be hungry again.'

Even so, the script was an excellent blueprint on which to work and Howard reluctantly agreed to travel to California. He knew from experience that Hollywood was a crazy place and he had further proof of that as soon as he arrived. Selznick was currently shooting *The Prisoner of Zenda* which had run into some script problems. Surely Howard could rewrite a few scenes. . . .

Eventually Selznick's mind focused on *GWTW* and the two men got down to work. Howard preferred to sit quietly in a chair and talk things over. Selznick liked to act everything out—a trait he shared with Mayer and other moguls—and walked around the room waving his arms and acting everyone's part. They argued, sulked and compromised well into the night for weeks on end until Selznick gave up. He had too many things pressing in on him and, somehow, the script

suddenly seemed less important than all the other concerns such as money, casting and technical matters. Howard returned to his farm and the script, by now a palimpsest decipherable only by Selznick, was shelved.

But when, many months later, Selznick had cast Rhett Butler and was faced with the shock of a shooting schedule with start and completion dates, he turned once again in earnest to the script. He decided that a change of scenery would be conducive to creative endeavour and chose the island of Bermuda. Since Howard and Margaret Mitchell were unwilling to join him, Selznick hired Jo Swerling, a Russian immigrant who had recently scripted Selznick's *Made for Each Other* (1938). In Bermuda Selznick and Swerling hacked into Howard's work until both men realized they were getting nowhere. From

Cameraman, Lee Garmes

Bermuda on 11 November 1938 Selznick cabled Kay Brown: 'Understand Oliver Garrett's play is a terrible flop so should be able to buy him cheaply. Want Garrett do continuity certain sequences, maybe only few, maybe throughout picture. If price right, would want him to familiarize himself with book and script and prepare work on my arrival in New York, probably also *en route* home and at studio.'

On 28 November 1938 Garrett and Selznick took the train across the United States to Hollywood. It was a five-day trip and nothing much was accomplished. Garrett returned to New York and in the ensuing weeks, as the start date

Technicolor cameraman, Ray Rennahan (seated to the right of the camera)

approached, Selznick hired any number of writers—maybe a dozen —to get the story into shape and down to a realistic length. One of those writers who laboured fruit-lessly for a day or two was the celebrated novelist F. Scott Fitzgerald who seems to have been hired more for his critical observa-tions than for his abilities as a scriptwriter which were, to say the least, unrealized. Fitzgerald offered the opinion that Sidney Howard's script was as good as Selznick could possibly hope for.

All the troubles that lay ahead had their basis in the script. By the time Selznick returned to Hollywood from Bermuda there were more pressing matters to attend to. He had left behind a crew of technicians and now they wanted his undivided attention. The script, however shapeless, just had to do; it was as if he hoped he might will the picture to completion without one. Perhaps he wondered why he was making the picture at all, since Margaret Mitchell's novel had already delighted millions of readers. Selznick's *GWTW* could only be a poor facsimile; he was a slave to its characters, its plot, its highlights and its flaws. This was not movie-making, it was painting by numbers. But that painting would be of unusual quality.

Selznick had decided to assemble the finest technicians in Hollywood and make *GWTW* as visually impressive as money and technology would allow. For his director of photography he chose Lee Garmes, a veteran of the silent cinema and the man who photographed Marlene Dietrich, for director Josef von Sternberg. Garmes was in Britain working for producer Alexander Korda when the call from Selznick came. 'You could have knocked me over with a feather,' said Garmes, 'because I thought most of the picture had been finished. I'd been

Production Designer, William Cameron Menzies

reading about it in the press for months! I got my agent to accept, and I cut my salary almost in half to do it. When I got to Hollywood [in January 1938] I realized the picture hadn't been started—except for the Atlanta fire shot by Ray Rennahan.'

Selznick had decided to make *GWTW* in Technicolor. Although many silent films had experimented with colour and tinting processes, it was not until Rouben

At the hospital Dr Meade says Scarlett must cope on her own—he can't leave his patients.

Mamoulian's *Becky Sharp*, released in 1935, that full three-strip Technicolor was used for a live-action feature film. Since virtually all of Hollywood's lighting camera-men, including Garmes, had little or no experience of colour, Technicolor had the studios well and truly buttoned up. They could dictate their own terms. Technicolor stipulated that one of their own cameramen and an assistant be assigned as technical advisers on every film which used the process. For *GWTW*, Technicolor assigned Paul Hill who was soon replaced by Ray Rennahan, plus an assistant.

A vast army of designers was also required to recreate the period. The sets and costumes were to be historically authentic, as long as they were suitably dramatic on screen. The chief art director was Lyle Wheeler, a long-time associate of Selznick's, and the chief costume designer was Walter Plunkett. There would be squabbles, of course, so Selznick hired the brilliant production designer William Cameron Menzies as the ultimate arbiter on all things visual. Menzies had designed the spectacular sets for Douglas Fairbanks's two-strip Technicolor adventure *The Thief of Baghdad* (1924), and had directed, as well as designed, *Things to Come* (1936) for Korda. Menzies would become Selznick's greatest creative asset, whose set designs, storyboards, ideas for photography and his direction of several key sequences would give *GWTW* its visual coherence. As long as Menzies was around, cameramen, writers and directors could come and go as they or Selznick pleased. And they did.

Selznick's technical team was dispatched to the Old South for research. Like Cukor, who had toured the area looking for possible Scarletts, they had the services of Margaret Mitchell as guide and key to local museums and archives. But they returned convinced that there were no suitable locations and that the authentic architecture was not grandiose enough for a movie. Mitchell had always envisaged Tara, the family home of the O'Haras, to be solid and stable but hardly opulent. She showed them examples of what she had in mind. 'I am sure they were dreadfully disappointed,' she wrote after Cukor and Plunkett's visits. Selznick wanted something grander, a kind of ante bellum Beverly Hills. If it could not be found then it had to be built, so the decision was made to shoot the film almost entirely on the backlot. Some authentic Georgian vistas were shot for the opening credit titles, but southern California stood in for northern Georgia for the major exterior sequences. Tara, Twelve Oaks and Atlanta would all be constructed on Washington Boulevard in Los Angeles—standard procedure at that time.

There was only one Rhett Butler—Clark Gable

Although Prissy has boasted that she has attended lots of births, she now says she knows 'nothin' about birthin' babies'. Angry and scared Scarlett slaps her, but gathers her wits and attends to Melanie. Thus, Ashley's son comes into the world.

Shooting the film on the backlot would virtually transform *GWTW* into a special effects picture of unprecedented scale, requiring a large number of matte paintings southern landscapes and interior sets of scenic backdrops as well as interior sets. Menzies was especially valuable here—after all, he made Douglas Fairbanks fly on a magic carpet and had created the twenty-first century. To supervise the effects Selznick hired Jack Cosgrove, whose magic would turn the most lavish ideas on paper into celluloid reality. Things were beginning to come together, to take shape; there was a movie in sight and through Menzies' storyboards Selznick had a clear idea of what it would look like. Except that, after a year, there was still no start date, no

Errol Flynn

script, no money and no cast.

Throughout this year Selznick had received a flood of mail which told him how the picture should be made. The writers may have disagreed on which actress should play Scarlett but, despite suggestions of Errol Flynn and Gary Cooper, there was virtual unanimity on who should play Rhett Butler—Clark Gable. Selznick knew it as well but the thought filled him with apprehension and dread because Gable was under contract to Louis B. Mayer and MGM. If David Selznick was the creative eminence behind *Gone With the Wind*, then Louis B. Mayer was the *eminence grise*. In the event, Gable was to provide more than just his services as an actor; with him came a great deal of money, as well as the reason why production could be postponed for as long as it took to find the right Scarlett O'Hara, Melanie, Ashley and other members of the cast.

In time, Gable would be known as 'The King' because for years he was indisputably the biggest male star in Hollywood. He was born William Clark Gable in Cadiz, Ohio, in 1901, the son of a farmer and oil worker. It seems he always wanted to act, but no one took him seriously. He subsidized himself with labouring jobs until, at the age of twenty-one, he joined a travelling theatre troupe in Oregon. The troupe was run by the actress Josephine Dillon, who was fourteen years older than Gable. They married in 1924 and settled in Hollywood.

Gary Cooper

Mrs Gable coached her handsome, young husband but secured him no nobler work than a movie extra. Gable left his wife (they divorced in 1930) and went to Broadway where he scored some modest successes. One of his plays, *The Last Mile*, travelled to Los Angeles and during its run Gable was tested by MGM, who turned him down. He also tested at Warner Brothers where producer Darryl F. Zanuck's verdict was, 'His ears are too big. He looks like an ape.' Despite these rather off-putting reactions, in the end Gable did get the role as the villain in a William Boyd western, *The Painted Desert*

(1931), and subsequently signed a two-year contract at MGM for $350 per week.

MGM badly needed a romantic male lead, someone who would look good beside the studio's extraordinary roster of actresses, including Joan Crawford, Greta Garbo, Jean Harlow and Norma Shearer. Since they were casting Gable in gangster pictures it took a little time for Mayer and Thalberg to realize that he was their man.

When Gable became romantically involved with Joan Crawford MGM tried to stop the affair, fearing that the unseemly gossip would undermine Crawford's career. The gossip-mongering, though, heightened Gable's appeal and audiences were becoming increasingly aware of this tall, raffishly handsome man with high cheekbones, cocked eyebrows, a pencil-thin moustache and a flashing smile who got Crawford, Garbo and Harlow in a romantic dither. He was not a 'Great Lover' or a preening Narcissus in the mould of silent stars like Rudolph Valentino or John Gilbert; Gable would rather slap a woman than whisper sweet nothings in her ear to get what he wanted. But unlike James Cagney in his psychotic gangster roles, Gable's violence was an expression of his own particular brand of macho love, not misogyny. Women loved his virility, his confidence and his heroism. So, too, did men. Gable's sense of humour and his rough-and-ready image deflected any jealousy of him from male audiences. To borrow a phrase of film critic Alexander Walker's, Gable was both king and commoner. It hardly mattered that Gable, in private life, was plagued by doubts about his career, his acting ability and his libido.

A movie star in those days was a slave—fabulously rich, pampered and protected by studio executives and publicists, but a slave all the same. Today, stars like Robert Redford, Dustin Hoffman and Meryl Streep—and their agents— exert tremendous power and can afford to make whatever films they want, whenever and by whomever they fancy. In 1930s' Hollywood the stars enjoyed a popularity unknown today, but they were not masters of their own careers.

In 1931 Gable made twelve pictures and by 1933 he had a seven-year contract and his salary had risen to $2500 per week. Although this was a lot of money, MGM were getting him cheap since Gary Cooper and Fredric March were earning more than twice that. Gable knew this and started to be 'difficult', refusing to make everything the studio threw at him.

Gable's displays of temperament were punished in 1934 when MGM loaned him out to the decidedly down-market Columbia Pictures for Frank Capra's comedy *It Happened One Night* (1934) opposite Claudette Colbert who was being similarly punished by Paramount. The result, much to Gable's delight and Mayer's chagrin, was an Academy Award. Gable returned to MGM and scored two of his greatest successes—as Fletcher Christian in *Mutiny on the Bounty* (1935), a part he hated since he thought his fans would laugh at him in knee-breeches, and as the cynical saloon owner who discovers heroism in *San Francisco* (1936), a role that has much in common with Rhett Butler.

By now Gable was wearing false teeth, earning $4500 a week and had the United States at his feet. He learned that David Selznick wanted him to play Rhett Butler and the thought terrified him because he knew the public would not accept anyone else in the role. 'Miss Mitchell had etched Rhett into the minds of millions of people,' Gable said later. 'It would be impossible to satisfy them all. Rhett was

simply too big an order. I didn't want any part of him.' The question was, though, would Louis B. Mayer loan him out?

Selznick's original thoughts of Errol Flynn or Ronald Colman quickly evaporated. In the autumn of 1937 there were only two possibilities: Gable or Gary Cooper, who was under contract to Sam Goldwyn. Like Gable, Cooper personified American ideals but his sex appeal was not as great. Selznick and Whitney approached Goldwyn who gave them a firm 'No'. It was Gable or nothing.

So Selznick went to the patriarch of MGM and his own father-in-law to discuss the cost of a bale of cotton called Clark Gable. Actually, the wily chief of MGM had predicted everything: he knew that Selznick would want Gable and he knew that, in one way or another, *Gone With the Wind* could not be made without MGM. Thalberg had recently died and Mayer alone was in charge. He always regretted the decision to turn down *GWTW*—it was precisely the kind of whipped cream and American apple pie he loved—so he began a discreet campaign to retrieve the situation. His head of publicity, Howard Strickling, fuelled the public's demand for Gable and even had the art department supply newspapers with drawings of Gable in Southern costume.

Mayer's offer came with plenty of strings attached. He would loan Gable at an agreed fee and would also invest $1.25 million—half the anticipated budget—in return for distribution rights and 50 per cent of the profits for the next five years. If Selznick baulked at this, Mayer had another and much less attractive proposition: Selznick would cease to become an independent producer and would make the film for MGM.

Selznick promised to think about it. He also had to consider another problem. Selznick pictures were released through United Artists, a distribution contract that would expire in 1939. The terms offered by Mayer stipulated distribution by MGM, so to avoid breach of contract with UA, he would have to delay production.

This delay suited Selznick down to the ground. He would encourage the national obsession with the casting in order to wait for Gable and prepare the picture thoroughly. It was not until 24 August 1938, a year later, that the contract, giving MGM distribution rights in return for Gable and a $1.25 million investment, was agreed and signed. Gable was to receive from Selznick his regular MGM salary of $4500 a week. To mollify Gable, who remained fearful of Rhett Butler, Mayer devised an added inducement. Separated from his second wife, Rhea Langham, Gable had fallen in love with the gifted comedienne Carole Lombard whom he wanted to marry. Divorcing Langham would be extremely expensive and messy, so Mayer, like a benevolent godfather, settled the matter with a bonus of $50,000, a third of which was to be paid by Selznick. Rhett Butler might lose Scarlett O'Hara but Clark Gable had won Carole Lombard.

The point of no return had finally arrived. *Gone With the Wind* was no longer merely a project in the air but something that had to go on the floor. Selznick could not delay it any longer. He had the money now, he had his crew he had his Rhett Butler and he thought the script would do. He was still without a Scarlett, but with a bravado and showmanship entirely typical of him, he decided to hold a party on Saturday, 10 December 1938. That night Atlanta would go up in flames.

Prissy is sent to Belle Watling's house of ill repute to ask for Rhett's help in moving Melanie and the child to Tara.

THE SEARCH FOR

SCARLETT

It is one of the greatest of all Hollywood stories and time and embellishment has not diminished its power and romance. It tells how David Selznick, grimy and exhilarated by the inferno that had started on his word, was touched on the arm by

The burning of Atlanta with stunt doubles

his brother Myron who said, 'David, I'd like you to meet Scarlett O'Hara.' Selznick gazed into the face of Vivien Leigh and saw ...who knows what?

Through the flames and his own distraction, perhaps just another actress, yet another possibility, a further screen test. A few days earlier he had lost Paulette Goddard, the actress he had decided would play Scarlett, because of the paranoia and hypocrisy of the country he loved. But now his mind was on the fire that raged still, he was worried about the stunt people and whether the cameras were working properly. But was there something else in the flickering face of this woman and in Myron's words? Was this beginning also the end? Was it not rather like a movie, a great scene that people would remember? And if it wasn't he could surely make it so. Facts are never as attractive as legends.

David Selznick would always remember the drama of that night. He said later, 'When my brother introduced her to me, the dying flames were lighting up her face. I took one look and knew she was right—at least right as far as her appearance went—and right as far as my conception of how Scarlett O'Hara looked. I'll never recover from that first look.'

It was an extraordinary night which entailed a vast amount of planning and not a small amount of risk. *GWTW* required some large-scale sets and room had to be found for them on the forty-acre backlot which, in late 1937, resembled an archaeological site for movie buffs. There were pieces of first-century Jerusalem, built for Cecil B. deMille's *The King of Kings* (1923), there was the high wall which defended the natives of Skull Island from King Kong, the ruins of *The Garden of Allah*, and other broken sets barely worth excavating. Lyle Wheeler spent hours in the backlot, working out the plan for the new sets and wondering when the

Rhett steals a horse and buggy and takes Scarlett, Melanie, the child and Prissy out of the besieged city. The army has destroyed the munitions stores and fire is spreading rapidly. Rhett makes his way through the conflagration, avoiding gangs of looters and joining the straggling lines of defeated soldiers. 'Take a good look, my dear,' he says to Scarlett. 'You can tell your grandchildren how you watched the Old South disappear one night.'

bulldozers would arrive. And then an ingenious idea occurred to him. These old sets, carefully dressed and photographed in the dark, could represent Atlanta. They would burn them down.

And so it was. Selznick loved the idea because it would be an occasion and make good copy for the newspapers. He would order a fire and play Napoleon with a megaphone and a helmet. They rehearsed all day, broke for dinner and lit the fuse at 8 p.m. With Cukor looking on, the sequence was directed by William Cameron Menzies and photographed by Ray Rennahan who had twenty-seven cameramen and seven Technicolor cameras under his control. The celebrated stuntman Yakima Canutt and stuntwoman Dorothy Fargo impersonated Rhett Butler and Scarlett O'Hara as they made their way through the inferno. The fire lit up the sky and, much to Selznick's delight, a rumour spread that MGM was ablaze.

Vivien Leigh

Although Selznick had not met Vivien Leigh before, she was not entirely unknown to him. In January 1937 she had been spotted by one of Selznick's talent scouts, Oscar Serlin, in *Fire Over England*, an Elizabethan drama in which she played Flora Robson's lady-in-waiting. On 3 February 1937 Selznick cabled Kay Brown and Serlin, 'I have no enthusiasm for Vivien Leigh. Maybe I will have, but as yet have never even seen a photograph of her. Will be seeing *Fire Over England* shortly, at which time will of course see Leigh.' Selznick never found the time to run the picture.

But Myron Selznick saw it, principally because Leigh was deeply in love with one of Myron's clients, the British actor Laurence Olivier and the star of the picture. Myron realized that Leigh had potential and perhaps even in the back of his mind was the idea she might be what David was looking for.

Scarlett O'Hara was in the forefront of Vivien Leigh's mind. She had read the novel and while she did not much like Scarlett, she recognized her as a great seven-course banquet of a part, as indeed had every actress who could read. Six thousand miles away in London, she plotted a course that would lead her to Hollywood and the attentions of David Selznick.

Vivien Leigh was born Vivian Mary Hartley in Darjeeling, India, in 1913. The hill station and tea plantations of Darjeeling, nestling in the shadow of the

Himalayas, was a favourite spot for the British middle and upper classes. Leigh was terribly English and terribly beautiful—pert, self-assured and ambitious.

She was educated in convents in Britain, France, Germany and Italy, married a barrister, briefly attended RADA and had a number of small roles in minor British films. Her break came when one of her stage performances was admired by the producer Alexander Korda who signed her to a two-year contract. She was idle for a year and then made *Fire Over England*. Leigh and Olivier fell passionately in love and separated from their respective spouses.

Olivier was a major star; his stage work had brought him national acclaim and his films brought him to a much wider public. His first experience of Hollywood was unfortunate; he was fired by MGM from *Queen Christina* (1933) as Garbo could not respond to him, but in 1938 he was offered the part of Heathcliff in William Wyler's adaptation of *Wuthering Heights* for Sam Goldwyn. Leigh decided to visit Olivier in Hollywood and sent an alluring photograph of herself to Myron Selznick. On the ocean liner she read Mitchell's novel again and committed Scarlett's most important speeches to memory.

One night Myron said to Olivier and Leigh, 'Would you like to go to a fire?' The next day Cukor gave her a reading of the scene in which she declares her love for Ashley Wilkes. Cukor loved her immediately—she had 'a kind of indescribable wildness about her' he said—and so did Selznick. Her English accent needed some extensive coaching but after further tests Selznick was satisfied that he had found the actress he was looking for. Cukor held a dinner at his elegant Regency-style mansion on Cordell Drive where he told Leigh that Scarlett O'Hara had been cast. 'I guess we're stuck with you,' he said. Leigh would receive $15,000—a paltry sum, but she was unknown—and a seven-year contract. Korda was placated and Olivier and Leigh were asked to live apart to preserve their moral integrity and to save Selznick from unwanted publicity.

His fears about casting an unknown British actress were unfounded. Leigh had no following in the United States so she could not divide the fans as an American actress might. He also received a tremendous boost when he realized that Leigh's casting was supported in the South. First and foremost, Leigh was not a Yankee and since

They all wanted to be Scarlett, including Bette Davis

the Americans had vanquished the British in the War of Independence, Southerners equated this with their own war of independence. It was a peculiar form of logic which Selznick readily subscribed to.

'She was not beautiful,' wrote Margaret Mitchell in the opening line of the novel, 'but men seldom realized it when caught by her charm as the Tarleton twins

were.' Every actress in Hollywood coveted the role—save, perhaps Greta Garbo, Mae West and Lassie (who was male anyway)—and Selznick exploited the fact. It gave him publicity and bought him the time to solve the Gable-MGM-UA complication. To coordinate the campaign he hired Russell Birdwell, a reporter for Hearst newspapers. Birdwell had an eye and an ear for a story and did not mind how much dirt he had to dig to find it. For $250 a week he had to keep the story boiling for two years.

and Katherine Hepburn . . .

Birdwell called a press conference to announce a nation-wide search for a young unknown actress to play Scarlett. Talent scouts would cover the country; no one with a pretty face would be overlooked. Charles Morrisson was allocated all points west of the Mississippi, Oscar Serlin was to cover the North and East and Max Arnow, accompanied by Cukor, the South. In the South they discovered the appropriately-named Alicia Rhett who was cast as India Wilkes, Ashley's grim and scheming sister, but no one else. Rumours abounded that men posing as Selznick talent scouts installed themselves in hotels and found women flocking to their rooms. In the end, Selznick spent an estimated $92,000 and Cukor shot twenty-four hours of test footage to little avail except publicity.

It was all patently absurd but the public lapped it up. Selznick easily justified the effort, the equivocation and the hype. 'A producer can only find and put over new personalities when he has patience, and the money for overheads, and the authority to refuse to be rushed into making his

and Southern Belle Tallulah Bankhead . . .

judgements. If you have to get somebody by Wednesday when shooting starts, you take the best available and cross your fingers and pray. The pressure for haste on *Gone With the Wind* was severe, but I knew that seventy-five million people would want my scalp if I chose the wrong Scarlett, and that there was no agreement on who, among all the girls in pictures, was the right Scarlett.'

Bette Davis actually came top of most of the polls that Birdwell organized.

Even Mrs Thalberg, Norma Shearer and Miriam Hopkins ... and Joan Crawford ... and Joan Bennett ... and Selznick's old flame Jean Arthur ... and Irene Dunne ... all saw themselves as Scarlett

To coin a phrase, Davis was not beautiful, but men, caught by her anger and her dominance, seldom realized it. She was a great actress and a major star at Warner Brothers. Jack Warner made Selznick an offer of Bette Davis, Errol Flynn, Olivia de Havilland and 25 per cent of the profits. Selznick found that easy to refuse but Davis still hankered for the part. She never tested as Scarlett O'Hara; instead, she made a complete movie—William Wyler's *Jezebel*, in which she played a Southern belle who loses her beau, Henry Fonda, because she wears a scarlet gown to a ball. Selznick was furious and wrote angry letters to Warners, claiming they had deliberately lifted scenes from Mitchell's novel and had exploited Selznick's own publicity for *GWTW*. Jack Warner thanked Selznick for his interest and Davis won an Academy Award. But at least *Jezebel* had proved that Civil War pictures were capable of making rather more than a nickel.

Katharine Hepburn refused to make a test. She was a close friend of George Cukor and, of course, a brilliant actress. She had tried to get RKO to buy *GWTW* for her and when that failed she began a campaign of her own which ignited when Margaret Mitchell seemed to endorse her candidacy. Mitchell had simply said she liked Hepburn in Cukor's *Little Women* (1933) and thought she looked pretty in hoop skirts. Mitchell quickly apologized for giving any impression that she preferred Hepburn. Selznick, though, was adamant. He thought Hepburn lacked sex appeal and her current box-office ranking was extremely low. At the

Rhett stops the buggy at the turn-off to Tara. His cynicism has been replaced by a sense of idealism and shame. He will be enlisting in the army to be present at the last battle. Scarlett is furious he will not take her all the way to Tara.

same time he was pondering over Leslie Howard as Ashley. He thought that if he cast Howard and Hepburn 'we can have a lovely picture for release eight years ago'. While Hepburn fell at the first fence, Howard would last the distance.

The first important star to test for *GWTW* was Tallulah Bankhead. If Mae West's sexuality was a cartoon, Tallulah's was for real; no one could sulk or pout quite like her. She was born in Alabama and had a genuine Southern accent, ripened by bourbon and five packs of Chesterfields a day. She also had something else in her favour: she was the former lover of Jock Whitney. But her tests, directed by Cukor, were unsatisfactory. She was convincing in later scenes, when Scarlett runs her own life and everyone else's, but Selznick felt she was unable to portray the younger and innocent Scarlett. Then Selznick wanted her to play Belle Watling, the warm-hearted, charitable madam of the bordello who 'comforts' Rhett Butler when Scarlett won't sleep with him. Selznick did not dare offer Bankhead this consolation prize. Instead, he asked Kay Brown 'to brave the lioness's den. As a disappointed Scarlett she's likely to bite your head off—and for God's sake don't mention my name.' Kay Brown never acted on the memo.

Bankhead, aged thirty-four, was too old to play Scarlett who is sixteen at the start of the film. But age is no deterrent or obstacle to actresses who always think they are twenty-two and have make-up artists to prove it. Irving Thalberg's wife, Norma Shearer, had played Juliet at the age of thirty-six for director George

He pulls her off the buggy. 'I love you,' he says, 'in spite of you and me and the whole silly world going to pieces around us. I love you because we're alike, bad lots both of us ... Scarlett you're a woman sending a soldier to his death ... Kiss me.'

Lucille Ball auditioned as Scarlett

Cukor and she was tipped to play Scarlett. So too were Miriam Hopkins, Joan Crawford, Joan Bennett, Jean Arthur and Irene Dunne. All of them were into their thirties and none passed Selznick's scrutiny, though some, especially Hopkins and Jean Arthur (a former flame of his) got him thinking seriously. Lucille Ball tested and so did MGM's new starlet Lana Turner. Cukor was seeing so many actresses it all became a blur.

The Ashley problem could not be postponed any longer. In many ways it is the most difficult role in the film and, in terms of narrative, the most important, for it is Scarlett's love for Ashley that initiates much of the drama. Ashley—self-absorbed, disconsolate and trying to preserve his notion of honour—crops up at key moments, caught hopelessly between his wife Melanie and the adoring Scarlett. He is the equivalent of Pierre in *War and Peace*, the shattered romantic, and might have been a superb role for Henry Fonda who eventually played Pierre in 1956. But Selznick never considered Fonda. It was Leslie Howard all along.

Cukor had tested Robert Young, Jeffrey Lynn and Lew Ayres, while Selznick's wife recommended Ray Milland. Melvyn Douglas gave what Selznick thought was 'the first intelligent reading we've had', though he was rejected as being too 'beefy' for Ashley. Selznick kept coming back to Howard, the British stage actor and matinée idol who had become a Hollywood star. Howard, though, despised the

And starlet Lana Turner ...

trappings of stardom and wanted to write, produce and direct. He hated the character of Ashley, refused to read Mitchell's novel and thought he was too old for the part. Selznick offered him a wig, youthful make-up and a job as associate producer on *Intermezzo*, another property he was developing to star his new Swedish discovery, Ingrid Bergman. Howard accepted.

As Scarletts came and went like the tide, other actors stayed. Hattie McDaniel was cast as Mammy, Butterfly McQueen was Prissy, the stupid and

Melvyn Douglas tested as Ashley. Robert Young tested as Ashley. Jeffrey Lynn tested as Ashley. Lew Ayres tested as Ashley. Ray Milland tested as Ashley. Lesley Howard got the role and hated it.

hysterical maid, Thomas Mitchell was Scarlett's father, Ward Bond was the Union soldier, Ona Munson was Belle Watling, Evelyn Keyes and Ann Rutherford were Scarlett's sisters, and Rand Brooks and Carroll Nye were Scarlett's short-lived husbands.

For the part of Melanie, the woman with so much heart it finally breaks, Selznick had tested several actresses. When Joan Fontaine was under consideration she protested that she thought she should play Scarlett and recommended her sister, Olivia de Havilland, as a potential Melanie. De Havilland was invited to Selznick's house where she read through a scene with Cukor who played Scarlett with considerable aplomb. 'I'm sure it was his performance that got me the part,' said de Havilland.

Paulette Goddard was initially Selznick's favourite for Scarlett

The search for Scarlett, though, was seemingly without end. Selznick's most prolonged and serious dalliance was with Paulette Goddard. In looks and temperament she seemed to spring from the pages of Mitchell's novel. She worked hard, giggled and was coached at home by the man she was in love with, Charles Chaplin. She was inexperienced as an actress—her biggest role had been in Chaplin's *Modern Times* which, even in 1936, was a silent picture—but her confidence was overwhelming. She would develop in the role as Scarlett herself develops from a flighty teenager into a manipulative businesswoman.

Goddard became Selznick's favourite. Everyone liked her spirit and admired her beauty. She did test after test and responded well to her dialogue coach, Will Price, who gave her a Southern accent. The gossip columnist Louella Parsons had even started to call her Scarlett O'Goddard. Selznick's search had ended and Goddard was on the verge of being signed.

Then the moral majority, inflamed by the gossip columns, made its presence felt and woe betide a producer who chooses to ignore it. Letters from Women's Clubs poured in to the Selznick studios threatening to boycott the film if Chaplin's mistress played their (far from pure) heroine. Selznick buckled under the strain and cancelled her next and possibly final test. Such were the times in which they lived and loved, compromised and capitulated.

The search for another actress was resumed until that night, a few days later, when Atlanta burned and Vivien Leigh's eyes blazed with the fire of Scarlett O'Hara. She later recalled the first of her many screen tests. 'When I put that costume on it was still warm from the previous actress.'

Rhett kisses her violently, but Scarlett breaks free of his embrace, slaps him and says she hopes he will be blown into a million pieces.

THE CUKOR SITUATION

AND OTHERS

It was 8 a.m. on 26 January 1939. The flag of the Confederacy flew in front of the Selznick studio and George Cukor called, 'Action!' They were shooting the first scene in the picture and the first scene in the novel on the porch of Tara with Vivien Leigh and the Tarleton twins. Everyone was nervous but by lunchtime the cameraman, Lee Garmes, and Cukor seemed satisfied. Then the light faded and they went indoors to shoot the dressing scene with Leigh, Hattie McDaniel and Butterfly McQueen.

The next day David Selznick was a worried man. He had already spent over a million dollars, more than a third of the budget (which was now $2.8m) and had two scenes completed—two scenes he didn't like. Selznick knew the first scene would have to be re-shot and convinced himself that the shrill quality of Leigh's performance was simply due to nerves. But the second sequence bothered him a great deal. Cukor's pacing was slow; he seemed to be paying more attention to incidental details than moving the story along. Worst of all, Cukor had decided to

give Butterfly McQueen an extra line of dialogue. Since it was taken straight from the novel, Selznick could not question its authenticity but he could—and did—question Cukor's authority.

On the other hand, Vivien Leigh and Olivia de Havilland adored their director. He was attentive and considerate and discussed their roles in great depth, encouraging them to express their own attitudes towards the characters they were playing. It was a genuine collaboration that allowed Leigh to underplay the bitchiness in Scarlett and accentuate the more sympathetic aspects of the character. Cukor put up with Selznick's criticisms and got on with the job he was being paid for.

Selznick insisted on control of the script

The road to Tara is long and desolate: there are units of Yankees to avoid, buzzards picking at the bones of dead horses and even dead soldiers who lie by the roadside. There is intense heat which brings massive storms. There is nothing to eat and the horse is dying of exhaustion. But still Scarlett urges herself on.

Things did not improve when Clark Gable arrived for work on 31 January 1939. In deference to the star's importance and his liking for masculine surroundings, Selznick gave Gable a large dressing room furnished like a hunting

lodge. Despite these attempts to make Gable feel at home, he still felt like a late arrival at a dinner party. He was nervous, totally unprepared for his role, and he knew that Cukor had become very close to Leigh and de Havilland.

Gable's first day on the set did little to boost his confidence. It was the spectacular scene of the bazaar when the recently widowed Scarlett scandalizes Atlanta society by agreeing to dance with Rhett Butler. Gable was not Fred Astaire so Cukor had a revolving platform attached to the camera to improve his waltzing. The great romantic star naturally felt exposed. He respected Cukor's talent but found it impossible to relate to a director who called him 'darling', gossiped like a society hostess, fussed over the actresses' hairdos and insisted that the star adopt a Southern accent. Gable only had one performance—Clark Gable—and it seemed that was not what Cukor wanted.

After ten days of shooting, Selznick, burdened with all kinds of worries, had become a mass of contradictions. He had said repeatedly that *GWTW* could not be made in a factory. It was not a production-line model like a Ford or a Chrysler, or even a Cadillac. *GWTW* was to be a Rolls-Royce, handcrafted from start to finish. Yet now he was constantly urging Cukor to get a move on. It seemed he would be satisfied with a Cadillac after all. Selznick was also alarmed by Cukor's cavalier attitude to the script; the director was adding lines and even speeches whenever and wherever he wanted. In order to eliminate these

They reach Twelve Oaks, a shattered shell that houses only memories . . .and a dairy cow. 'Oh, Ashley,' says Scarlett to herself,' I'm glad you're not here to see this.'

'projection room surprises' and have control over every scene, Selznick ordered Cukor to arrange rehearsals which Selznick would attend. Quite apart from outraging Cukor and undermining his authority, Selznick's constant revision of the script made rehearsals virtually impossible since no one knew what lines they would read the next day. Selznick also found fault with the costumes, the photography and the art direction. He criticized everything and everyone and let it be known that he thought the results so far were technically inferior to the colour films being made at Warner Brothers for half the cost.

Although Gable never officially complained to Selznick about Cukor, his general discomfort was known at MGM and, of course, Gable knew this would filter through to Selznick. Gable's loan-out contract included a clause which absolved MGM of any responsibility should Gable, for whatever reason, 'refuse to perform'. In today's parlance, it was 'pay or play'. Aware of Gable's misgivings and conscious of his own considerable stake in the picture, Louis B. Mayer entered the debate, expressing to Selznick his view that Cukor seemed to be painting a miniature rather than a full-scale mural. Selznick realized that, one way or another, Cukor would have to go.

There had been an earlier 'Cukor situation', as Selznick called it, which had been resolved. Before starting work on *GWTW*, Cukor had directed what is probably Garbo's best film, *Camille* (1936), for Irving Thalberg at MGM. Cukor

Tara. It is dark and ominous but then, as if by a miracle, the clouds drift apart and the full moon lights up the house— overgrown but untouched, still home, still Tara!

regarded himself, with some justification, as a great director, one of Hollywood's élite. And now he had been assigned to direct the most publicized and possibly the most important film in Hollywood's history.

In those days directors did not spend years on a project; they approved the script, made a few amendments, directed the actors and left the editing to the editors, then got on with their next movie. But *GWTW* was different, so Cukor happily immersed himself in research and endless screen tests. For a studio director this kind of preparation was a rare luxury. But Selznick began to think that Cukor had become an 'expensive luxury'. He voiced his concern in a confidential memo to Dan O'Shea, vice-president of Selznick International, on 21 September 1938. 'George has been with us now for a long time and we have yet to get a picture out of him.' What Selznick wanted was Cukor's undivided attention on the pre-production of *GWTW*, as well as another picture to justify his salary of $4000 a week, which was only $500 less than Gable's. 'We are in danger actually of winding up paying [Cukor] about $300,000 for his services on *GWTW*. . . . We are a business concern and not patrons of the arts.'

Selznick had offered other films to Cukor, including *A Star Is Born* (which Cukor would remake in 1954) and *Intermezzo*. Cukor turned them both down because he was committed to the research and the tests for *GWTW* and because he had a reputation for only making pictures with actors he liked. In 1938 he did consent to being loaned out to Columbia for *Holiday*, with Cary Grant and Katharine Hepburn, and then to Paramount for *Zara* with Claudette Colbert and Herbert Marshall. This seemed to mollify Selznick; *Holiday* and *Zara* were not Selznick pictures—nor were they Cukor's best—but at least someone else was footing the bill.

Then in November 1938 Selznick received a panic call from Louis B. Mayer. MGM's elaborate musical, *The Wizard of Oz*, was in trouble and the director, Richard Thorpe, had been fired. Could Cukor replace him? Selznick insisted that he could, so Cukor worked on *The Wizard of Oz* for two disastrously unhappy days until, irony of ironies, he was replaced by Victor Fleming. The first 'Cukor situation' had proved to be a storm in an expensive teacup.

But now, barely two weeks into the filming of *GWTW*, another 'Cukor situation' had blown up and pieces of shrapnel were flying in all directions. Things came to a head on 7 February 1939 when, in the presence of Selznick, Cukor was shooting the scene of the birth of Melanie's baby. The dim-witted slave girl, Butterfly McQueen, was to say to Scarlett, 'If you put a knife under the bed it cuts the pain in two.' Cukor wanted her to deliver the line in an agitated, almost hysterical way, as befitted her character. Selznick disagreed; he wanted McQueen to deliver the line calmly. Selznick won the day and Cukor knew he was finished.

On the day before shooting started, Selznick sent a memo to Jock Whitney in an attempt to reassure his partner that there was a script and that everything would go well. Selznick wrote, 'It is so clearly in my mind that I can tell you the picture from beginning to end, almost shot by shot.' William Cameron Menzies' storyboards were Selznick's guidelines to the picture and the script was entirely in his head. He had become, in effect, the director, writer and producer. Cukor, at odds with Selznick, Gable and the script, found his position untenable.

On Monday 13 February 1939 *Variety* and the *Hollywood Reporter* carried an announcement that George Cukor had left *Gone With the Wind* '. . . as a result of a series of disagreements over many of the individual scenes'. Selznick added a personal note: 'Mr Cukor's withdrawal is the most regrettable incident of my rather long producing career, the more so because I consider Mr Cukor one of the very finest directors it has ever been the good fortune of this business to claim. I can only hope that we will be so fortunate as to be able to replace him with a man of comparable talents.' In 1957 Selznick would fire John Huston from the production of Ernest Hemingway's *A Farewell to Arms*, reiterating in his long memo to Huston what he had said regarding Cukor's dismissal from *GWTW*: 'I can only say what I said to Cukor: "If this picture is going to fail, it must fail on *my* mistakes, not yours".' However, the dust settled and Selznick and Cukor would remain the greatest of friends—'a tribute to both of us', said Cukor later. And when it was all over, when the tears of triumph washed away the tears of anger and recrimination, Cukor would send Selznick a cable to wish him well.

Selznick was concerned that Cukor should go straight into another picture and not into a sort of limbo where he might brood privately and face the scorn of the trade press. Before the news of Cukor's departure from *GWTW* was announced, Mayer agreed to let Cukor direct *The Women* (1939) and re-assigned its director, Ernst Lubitsch, to Greta Garbo's first comedy, *Ninotchka* (1939). Both films turned out to be huge successes. The old Hollywood establishment—membership of which Selznick had now fully earned by showing that he valued a production more than personal friendship—had smoothed over the joins. Mayer and Selznick were relieved and so too was Clark Gable.

Replacement director, Victor Fleming

However, several of the production personnel were unhappy about the turn of events. The cameraman, Lee Garmes, who saw eye-to-eye with Cukor on the way the film should look, now found his own position threatened. But most of all, Vivien Leigh and Olivia de Havilland were shattered when they heard the news of Cukor's departure. In the months ahead they were to maintain their collaboration with Cukor by secretly visiting his house on Sundays where they would read their lines, discuss their roles and benefit from Cukor's advice and understanding. As Leigh said later, 'George was my last hope of ever enjoying the picture.' Everything was to change now, and not necessarily for the worse.

Victor Fleming was directing *The Wizard of Oz* and was within a month of completion. He had taken over from Richard Thorpe and George Cukor and turned the immensely complicated production into a well-oiled machine. Although he was totally out of his element amid the fairytale sets, tin men, munchkins and Judy Garland, Fleming knew how to get a show on the yellow-brick road to success. No one, least of all Fleming himself, would regard him as an artist who favoured particular

Overleaf: But tragedy lurks within. Scarlett's mother has died of typhoid and Scarlett's father is grief-stricken, refusing to believe it, his will to live gone. Scarlett's sisters are upstairs recovering from fever, and the slaves, Mammy and Sam, wander aimlessly about. The family fortune is now worthless and there is nothing to eat. Even Scarlett, for a moment at least, is crushed with defeat.

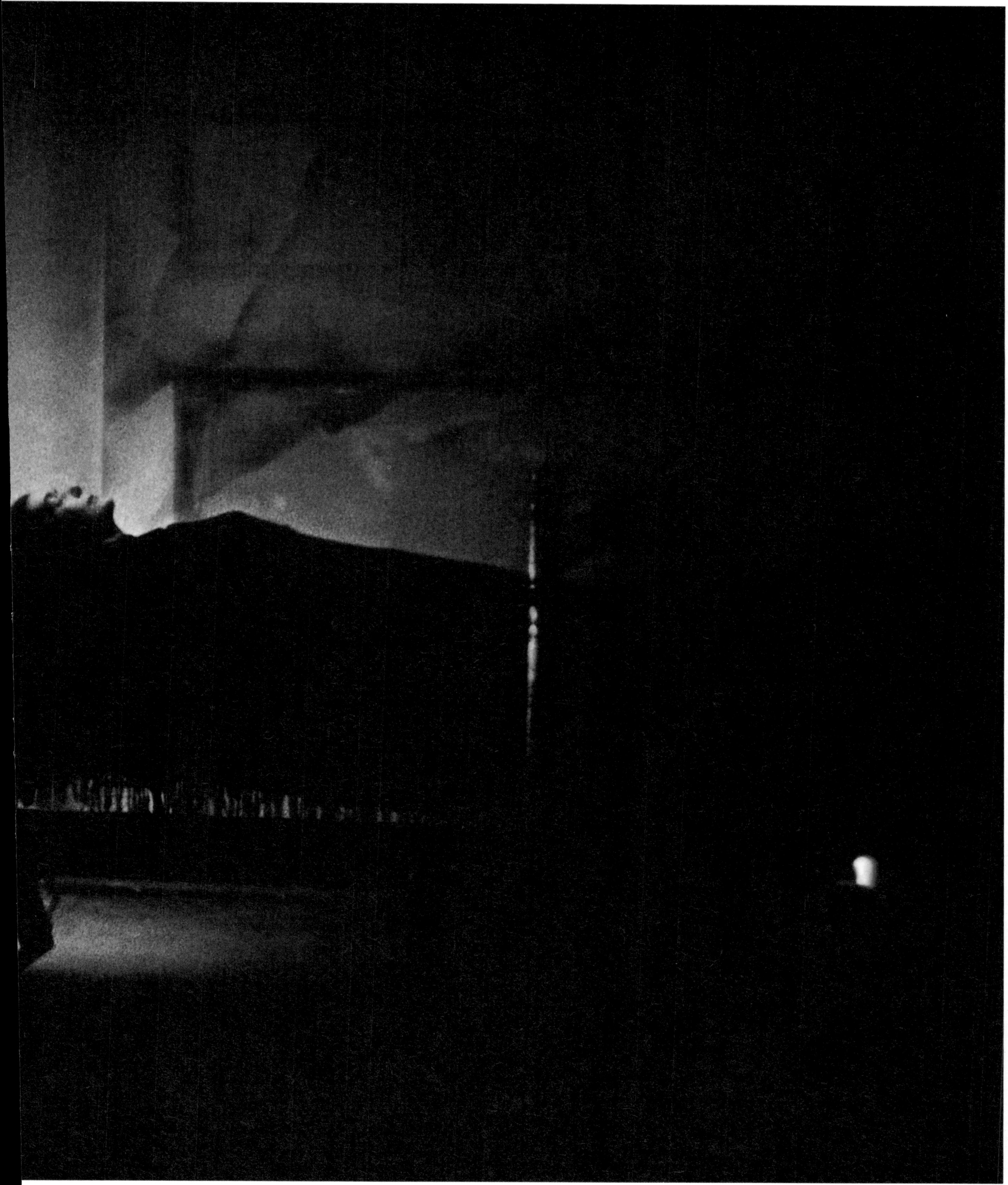

themes or jealously guarded his creative autonomy. At the same time, he was not a hack. He was a true Hollywood professional, serious about his work and modest about his achievements.

He was born in Pasadena in 1883 and entered films in 1910 as an assistant cameraman, working for D. W. Griffith and Allan Dwan, before making his directorial debut in 1919. His silent pictures, including versions of Joseph Conrad's *Lord Jim* (1925) and Samuel Butler's *The Way of All Flesh* (1927), revealed a significant talent, while his western, *The Virginian* (1929), catapulted Gary Cooper into decades of stardom.

Fleming signed with MGM in 1932 and scored an early success with *Red Dust* with Gable, Jean Harlow and Mary Astor. Set on a rubber plantation, it was just the kind of gutsy, sexy melodrama that Fleming excelled in and which set up the kind of dramatic structure (echoed in *GWTW*) that audiences adored: Gable torn between the recklessness of Harlow and the demure humanity of Astor. Fleming's subsequent films, *Bombshell* (1933), one of the greatest movies about Hollywood, *Treasure Island* (1934) with Spencer Tracy, and *Test Pilot* (1938) with Gable, were all equally successful and made him one of MGM's highest paid contract directors.

When he was faced with the first 'Cukor situation' Selznick had considered bringing in Fleming at once and offering him a contract. But now, faced with another and much more serious 'Cukor situation', Selznick turned first to King Vidor since he was aware that Fleming was embroiled in *The Wizard of Oz*. Vidor, an acknowledged master of spectacle and intimate drama, might have been Selznick's best choice all along. But Vidor was unwilling to take over from Cukor and submit himself to Selznick's constant supervision. (When Vidor did finally work for Selznick, on *Duel in the Sun* in 1946, he walked off the set after two months' shooting, leaving Selznick to direct the actors himself until a replacement was found.)

Selznick knew that Fleming was Clark Gable's preferred director. They had worked together on two films and were close buddies, going on extended hunting and fishing trips together. So Selznick was obliged to seek the favour of Louis B. Mayer yet again. The far from cowardly lion of MGM was in a generous mood, agreeing to Selznick's request on the condition that Fleming was happy with the arrangement. In fact, Fleming was exhausted with work and was looking forward to a holiday. Only loyalty to Gable made him accept the assignment. Fleming's place on *The Wizard of Oz* was taken by King Vidor.

Fleming arrived at the Selznick studios on 17 February 1939 and was immediately shown Cukor's footage. It amounted to twenty-three minutes, of which only thirteen had received Selznick's full approval. The rest would have to be re-shot by Fleming. At the end of the screening Selznick received a surprise. 'David,' said Fleming, 'your script is no fucking good.'

No one had spoken to Selznick like that before and it was the last thing he wanted to hear. Fleming knew that Selznick was writing the script himself and decided to go straight for the jugular. Suddenly, Cukor's much more politely expressed reservations were justified since Fleming was an objective outsider. It was a critical moment and with one eye on common sense and another on the flamboyant gesture, Selznick rose to it superbly. At a cost of $10,000 a day, *Gone With the Wind* was closed down. The press, once so supportive, turned into cynics

For a moment she behaves like a starving animal, pulling a radish from the red earth and being instantly sick. But then her inner reserves of pride, resolve and strength take over, pulling her to her feet. 'As God is my witness, as God is my witness, they're not going to lick me. I'm going to live through this and when it's all over I'll never be hungry again. No, nor any of my folk! If have to lie, steal, cheat or kill, as God is my witness, I'll never be hungry again!'

overnight. *GWTW* became known as 'Selznick's folly'.

Selznick turned immediately to the writer Ben Hecht who had scripted the Fredric March–Carole Lombard comedy *Nothing Sacred* for him in 1937. Hecht had also scripted *Scarface* (1932) and *Gunga Din* (1939) and, with his partner Charles MacArthur, he was the author of *The Front Page* (1931), as well as *Wuthering Heights*, the movie which brought Laurence Olivier and Vivien Leigh to Hollywood. Hecht could write drama, comedy, romance, adventure; he could write hard-boiled, soft-boiled, over-easy, sunnyside-up, any way you wanted. He wrote quickly, brilliantly and regularly salvaged other writer's work without credit. Hecht was lured out to Hollywood from New York by a famous cable from writer Herman Mankiewicz: "Will you accept three hundred per week to work Paramount? All expenses paid. The three hundred is peanuts. Millions are to be grabbed out here and your only competition is idiots. Don't let this get around." Three hundred dollars was indeed peanuts. Selznick agreed to pay Hecht $15,000 for two weeks' work.

Hecht had not read Mitchell's novel so Selznick began to tell him the story. According to Hecht, 'It was as long as a whore's dream and as pointless.' In Hecht's bungalow at the Beverly Hill Hotel, Selznick and Fleming acted or hammed out the script until Hecht demanded to read Sidney Howard's original draft. Inevitably, he pronounced Howard's work to be excellent. Every day, from 7

a.m. to 2 a.m, Selznick and Hecht worked through the mass of material, tightening here, clarifying there, the studio doctor keeping them going with regular shots of benzedrine. After two weeks of this Hecht had had enough and took the train back home. Later, Selznick would play down Hecht's contribution and it seems that exhausting fortnight merely enabled him to see the problems more clearly. It did not, though, cure him of his habit of rewriting the script in the middle of the night.

Filming resumed under Victor Fleming's direction on 2 March 1939. Nine days later there was another crisis. Selznick was always finding fault with the visual quality of the material. He thought several sequences were dark and that the vivid colours of Menzies' storyboards were not being reproduced. In a memo to Henry Ginsberg, the general manager of the studio, he said, 'I would appreciate it if you would get together with Garmes and Rennahan and make clear that we simply cannot tolerate any more photography that is so dark as to bewilder an audience. . . . If we can't get artistry and clarity, let's forget the artistry.'

On 11 March 1939 Lee Garmes was fired. According to Garmes, 'We were using a new type of film, with softer tones, softer quality, but David had been accustomed to working with picture-postcard colours. He tried to blame me because the picture was looking too quiet in texture. I liked the look; I thought it was wonderful, and long afterwards [David] told me he should never have taken me off the picture. I did about a third of the picture; chronologically almost everything up to Melanie having the baby, except the fire which was done before I arrived. I never got screen credit.' Garmes was replaced by Ernest Haller who had been nominated for an Oscar for *Jezebel*.

Despite the 'Garmes situation', Fleming had brought about a transformation on the set. He was brusque, foul-mouthed and proud of his macho image. He was the kind of man who would concur with Kipling that 'a woman is only a woman, but a good cigar is a smoke'. He had everyone's respect, if not their affection. However much Vivien Leigh and Olivia de Havilland missed Cukor and disliked Fleming, their new director had injected fresh blood into their performances. Fleming was an expert judge of pace and *GWTW* was now hurrying along. And Gable was a much happier man. He had been given two days' leave to marry Carole Lombard in Arizona and, on the set under Fleming's direction, his performance began to develop. He was playing Clark Gable better than ever and now Vivien Leigh was being told to play, if not Jean Harlow in *Red Dust*, then at least Gable's kind of gal. The Civil War had given way to the war between the sexes.

After some twelve weeks of shooting the Selznick coffers were running dangerously low. The film was already over budget and with possibly another twelve weeks to go, followed by six months of post-production work, some drastic measures were needed. Whereas a major studio like MGM or Paramount had large reserves of capital as well as a constant flow of new releases to provide revenue, Selznick was working from film to film, each one hopefully paying for the next. But Selznick had no revenue, only expenditure; economies were out of the question.

His accountants calculated that the final production cost of *GWTW* might be as high as $4 million and that there was only enough money in the bank to cover three weeks of pay cheques. The Cukor and Garmes situations had received wide press attention and even now there reports of deep disagreements between Leigh and Fleming and that Fleming had even walked off the set and stayed home for

INTERMISSION

To split the Confederacy, to leave it crippled and forever humbled, the great invader marched, leaving behind him a path of destruction sixty miles wide, from Atlanta to the sea. But Tara had survived—to face the hell and famine of defeat and to be driven back to life by Scarlett's energy. Sometimes it was too much for her sisters who were unused to picking cotton like slaves.

three days. To make matters worse, the large-scale action sequences, including the Siege of Atlanta and Scarlett and Melanie's return to Tara, had yet to be filmed. Selznick had transformed *GWTW* from a sure-fire investment into a bad risk. No one on the East Coast would invest in 'Selznick's folly'.

Selznick realized he needed to convince existing investors that he was making a great masterpiece and a commercial blockbuster. He showed MGM a rough assembly of the first hour of the picture which duly impressed them. However, Louis B. Mayer and then Nick Schenck refused to underwrite the picture by an additional million. It was an obvious and inevitable tactic; knowing the film would have immense appeal and make millions, MGM hoped to assume complete control of the production by forcing Selznick into bankruptcy. But having fought so long a battle for his independence, Selznick had to look elsewhere for money.

Eventually, a complicated deal was worked out. The Whitney family, persuaded by Selznick's partner Jock Whitney, dug into their own fortune and raised one million dollars. Selznick then screened the rough assembly for Attilio Giannini and Joseph Rosenberg of the Bank of America. While the bankers were impressed by the footage, they were less impressed by Selznick's financial record; his last three films were failures and *GWTW* would have to gross many times more than any previous film simply in order to break even. Giannini agreed to invest $1.25 million on the condition that the loan was guaranteed by Whitney and in

Tara's enemies were not only poverty and hunger; a Union deserter invades the house and is shot dead by Scarlett who then finds in his clothes enough Yankee dollars to buy some food.

order for Whitney to agree to this stipulation, David and Myron Selznick were forced to give up their controlling stake in Selznick International.

The new infusion of money was like a shot of benzedrine to Selznick. He was under the most intense financial pressure and had an almost intolerable workload: he was re-writing the script daily, checking into details of design and costuming, viewing rushes, working with the editors, planning the marketing and advertising with MGM executives, attending to the needs of his stars, consulting with Fleming and Haller. And that was only his work on *GWTW*. He was also doing similar work on *Intermezzo*, which Leslie Howard was working on simultaneously, preparing Alfred Hitchcock's first Hollywood film, *Rebecca* (1940), and holding meetings on future productions. At the same time he was trying to hang on to his life as a husband and father.

In her autobiography Irene Selznick recalled those difficult months: 'The hours were the most punishing. They were insane and only made possible by benzedrine, in increasing amounts. Several nights he did without sleep. We so adjusted to each stage that, without our realizing it, the new stress became the norm, but the strain was cumulative. Perhaps it was only a movie, but on the home front it was more real than life. It was hard to keep a perspective—that movie had priority. I didn't know what a beating I was taking until David told me what guilt he felt when he looked at me.'

As soon as the capital arrived from Whitney and the Bank of America, Selznick launched into the big action scenes. For days on end Vivien Leigh was pitched into a maelstrom of hurtling wagons, cattle and a swarm of extras as the Old South took flight from General Sherman's approaching army. Selznick drove his cast and crew on; things must be better and quicker. When the body's natural adrenalin dried up, artificial stimulants were pumped into anyone who needed them. Then there were pills to make them sleep when they got home at night, if, indeed, they got home at all.

Selznick was not the only taskmaster; Vivien Leigh, too, was urging everyone on. Meanwhile, Clark Gable was relatively relaxed, Leslie Howard was diffident and above it all, convinced that his make-up and costume made him look like a gay doorman at the Beverly Wilshire Hotel, and Olivia de Havilland was coolly professional. But Leigh was excitable, irascible and impatient. Not only was she invaded by the spirit of Scarlett O'Hara, she was desperate to be reunited with Laurence Olivier who had finished *Wuthering Heights* and was now appearing on Broadway. At the end of each day's shooting, Leigh would insist they work on into the night. She was desperate to get the thing finished.

Selznick argued with Fleming incessantly about the script, the costumes, the Southern accents and the visuals. Sidney Howard had been recalled to California and worked until frustration overcame professional pride. Walter

Plunkett was berated for dressing Gable in working men's clothes and not the apparel of a star. The dialogue coach, Susan Merick, was criticized for inconsistency. And Selznick still felt the picture was visually disappointing, deciding that several sequences needed re-shooting on location. Acres of land in the valleys outside Los Angeles were tinted red to match the earth of north Georgia.

Vivien Leigh argued incessantly with Fleming over her performance. She knew it was the role of a lifetime—perhaps several lifetimes—and she knew that Fleming cared more for Gable and Rhett Butler. Fleming knew that he needed to create tension on the set between Scarlett and Rhett and he did so. However, it is a common failing of movie stars and, indeed, great actors, to see themselves and not the overall picture. They recall the experience rather than rate the result. In short, Fleming was extracting a great performance while Leigh was having a lousy time.

Inevitably, with cast and crew high or low on drugs and crippled by stomach cramps, something had to give. On 29 April 1939 it did. Fleming had been directing the scene in which Gable was to cry in Melanie's lap following Scarlett's miscarriage. Gable thought crying was a sissy thing to do that would not go down well with his fans. He walked off the set at 11.30 a.m. Eventually Fleming, Selznick, Leigh, de Havilland and even Carole Lombard would persuade Gable to shoot two versions of the scene, one wet and one dry, and convince him that the wet one was best. But that was some weeks away. After Gable stalked off, Fleming was in a rage and then had to contend with a combative Vivien Leigh. Fleming's nerve, body and ego snapped in two. He threw his script at her, told her she could 'shove it up your royal British ass', and quit the picture. It was left to an assistant director to break the news to Selznick. Fleming retreated to his house in Malibu and stared at the ocean. The studio press release claimed he had suffered a nervous breakdown.

Actually, Fleming had asked to be relieved two weeks earlier and was examined by studio doctors who thought he could continue working. Even so, Selznick laid plans to replace Fleming, if necessary, with Robert Z. Leonard or William Wellman. When Fleming did finally leave, his replacement turned out to be Sam Wood.

Replacement director, Sam Wood

Although the press made a great deal of Fleming's abrupt departure, it made little impact at the studio. He had given the film its own momentum, so much so that anyone could direct what remained. In a very real sense, it was Selznick and Leigh who were the driving forces of the film—indeed, its principal authors. But protocol and logistics demanded a director, and this time Louis B. Mayer and MGM offered Sam Wood, a veteran of silent movies, the director of the Marx Brothers comedies *A Night at the Opera* (1935) and *A Day at the Races* (1937). He had just completed *Goodbye Mr Chips* (1939). A competent craftsman, he was not in the same league as Cukor or even Fleming.

Although Selznick was pleased with Wood's work—the new director had shot the scene of Leslie Howard returning home from the war on leave, the meeting between Scarlett, Melanie and Belle Watling outside the church, and the scene with all the women as they wait for Gable to return from the raid on the shanty town—he realized that Wood's visual sense was not as strong as Fleming's. He also wondered how he might engineer Fleming's return and keep Wood on the payroll as well which would speed things up considerably. After all, he already had William Cameron Menzies directing exteriors in the San Fernando Valley and there were second units working on other sequences. What difference would another director make?

Taking with them a peace offering of two love birds in a cage, Selznick, Leigh and Gable visited Fleming in Malibu. Fleming said he thought *GWTW* would turn out to be 'the biggest white elephant of all time' but agreed to return to the fold. He also had no objections to Selznick's idea of retaining Sam Wood, though Fleming, of course, would be the senior director responsible for all the major sequences.

After two weeks' absence, Fleming duly returned and started work immediately on one of the film's most dramatic scenes—the end of Part One when, against the orange light of the Tara dawn, Scarlett makes her great speech of survival. It is a key moment in the picture, when Scarlett is transformed from a heedless flirt into a mature woman. The scene was shot in the San Fernando Valley several times over the next few weeks because the sun and the sky refused to perform properly. There was also something of a dispute when Leigh refused to retch after eating a raddish she had torn from the earth. The sound of the retching was dubbed in later, not by Leigh, who regarded such behaviour as unladylike, but by Olivia de Havilland.

There still remained the biggest shot in the picture, when Scarlett would walk through the wounded soldiers at the railway station in search of Dr Meade. Menzies had envisaged this as a single crane-shot, beginning on a close-up of Scarlett and slowly tracking back and craning upwards until the figure of Scarlett is all but lost in the panorama of suffering and defeat while, in close-up now, is the burned and tattered flag of the Confederacy. Drawing it as a storyboard was one thing; getting it on film was another.

The largest crane in Hollywood could extend to a maximum height of 25 feet. Menzies wanted a height of nearly 100 feet. Eventually the studio borrowed a crane from the Long Beach dockyard and had to construct a solid concrete ramp 150 feet long to support the crane and provide a smooth base for tracking. The script called for 1600 extras, but on the day Central Casting could only provide 800 people. The balance was made up in dummies whose limbs could be moved by real-life extras. The final result was one of the greatest shots in cinema history and when Margaret Mitchell's husband saw it he remarked, 'If we had had that many soldiers we'd have won the war.'

It was now May and five units were working simultaneously. Vivien Leigh might work with Sam Wood in the morning on a scene in Part Two, and work with Fleming in the afternoon on a scene in Part One. She might be needed for a shot with Menzies or with B. Reeves Eason, one of the second unit directors. The schedule was punishing but the end was now within sight. There were still problems, however: Leigh's regular outbursts, Howard's total indifference, Gable's ego . . . And then something extraordinary happened—they ran out of script.

On 27 June 1939 Victor Fleming directed the last scene in the picture. It was the moment when Gable packs his bags. Scarlett says to him, 'If you go, where shall I go, what shall I do?' and he replies, 'Frankly, my dear, I don't give a damn.' Then they shot Scarlett's response, not in the novel but added by Selznick, when she wonders how she might get Rhett back. Lying on that fateful crimson staircase she says, 'I won't think about it today. I'll think about it tomorrow . . .after all, tomorrow is another day.'

And that was that. It was a wrap. Selznick cabled Jock Whitney: 'Sound the siren. Scarlett O'Hara completed her performance at noon today. Gable finishes tonight or in the morning, and we will be shooting until Friday with bit people. I am going on the boat Friday and you can all go to the devil.'

T H E   B I G   S H O W

Riverside is a neat little town on the edge of the desert about sixty miles east of downtown Los Angeles. But in the American scheme of things, Riverside qualifies as a city within a county. Developed during the 1920s, there is a Spanish aura to the town and its leading hotel at the time, the Mission Inn, is one of California's greatest architectural masterpieces. Nowadays, Riverside is sufficiently far from Los Angeles to be snooty, yet near enough to be smothered in a blanket of smog. In the 1930s and 1940s the denizens of Riverside were a studio demographer's dream, so it was much favoured for sneak-previewing new pictures to gauge audience response.

Every studio head, producer and director will tell you about previews: how crucial they are and how meaningless. The opinion cards the audience fill in can be inspirational, depressing, accurate or seriously misguided. Previews can make or break a picture, tell a producer what works and what doesn't, if it's too long, boring, or just great as it is thank you very much. Irving Thalberg depended on previews since he never, or rarely, viewed rushes. He'd wait until a real audience saw the director's cut, assess the response, and then go to work, cutting, adding or ordering scenes re-shot. Previews were nerve-racking because, for the first time, there was an objective audience, unclouded by months or years of agonized writing, casting, designing, shooting, editing and scoring. For David Selznick that terrible, wonderful hour had arrived. It was time for *Gone With the Wind* to be unwound with all its secrets laid bare to the public gaze.

Selznick was usually hopeless at keeping secrets. He wanted all his friends and all Hollywood to see his creation and to share in his moment of glory. On this occasion, however, he knew that was impossible, but worst of all was the thought of the press getting so much as a glimpse of 'Selznick's folly'. Finally, he designated a date and told his aides to make all the arrangements. And so, on Saturday, 9 September 1939, Selznick gathered his wife, Jock Whitney, Hal Kern, twenty-seven cans of picture and twenty-seven cans of sound and turned right along Washington Boulevard.

It was a searingly hot afternoon as they left Los Angeles behind. No one talked in the car, or they all talked at the same time. Selznick was worried they were being followed. It was like a scene from an espionage picture. Eventually they came to the Fox Riverside Theater on the corner of 7th and Market. It was a typical movie house of the time, a lavish piece of Spanish Colonial Revival built by the partnership of Balch and Stanberry in 1928. The theatre was packed with people expecting to see Gary Cooper in *Beau Geste* and were then enduring the

Home from their lost adventure came the tattered cavaliers … Grimly they came hobbling back to the desolation that had once been a land of grace and plenty. And with them came another invader, more cruel and vicious than any they had fought—the carpetbagger.

supporting film, *Hawaiian Nights*. According to Irene Selznick, 'David, standing on the pavement, sent for the manager. As David introduced himself, the manager obviously jumped to the right conclusion because he threw out his arms, clearly promising anything, anything.'

In the theatre a title card flashed on to the screen: 'Special Announcement'. Then the manager walked on to the stage and read a prepared speech. He announced a studio preview, a very special preview. No, he wouldn't say what it was. Riverside audiences were accustomed to being used as guinea pigs and knew how the game was played. But as the manager continued it became clear that this was no ordinary preview. Could it possibly be? The manager was very grave; the picture is unusually long, you may make a phone call if you wish, no one else will be admitted into the theatre, if you leave you will not be re-admitted, the doors will be locked. Surely it must be!

It took a little time to get things organized. And then the curtains opened and the lights went down. Almost at once, Margaret Mitchell's name was up there. The main titles to the picture had not been completed and neither had the music. So Hal Kern had the art department design some evocative title cards and ran Alfred Newman's fanfaring music from *The Prisoner of Zenda* over them. It was pandemonium and the applause and the cheering might have carried on the desert wind to Hollywood itself. The Selznick party broke into tears. In time, so would the audience as well.

That night, uniquely, *Gone With the Wind* ran for four hours and twenty-five minutes. At first you could have heard a pin drop and then came the applause, engulfing the auditorium like a tidal wave. 'Don't cut a minute', 'The best picture I have ever seen', 'Vivien Leigh is one of the most super colossally great actresses I have ever seen', 'Every adult man and woman should be required to see it'. The preview cards were extraordinary, fulsome in their praise. Selznick now knew that *GWTW* was as good as he thought it was. All that remained was to finish the picture in time for the première.

After Selznick sent his cable telling everyone they could go to the devil, re-takes had started almost immediately. Vivien Leigh had flown to New York and Olivier had managed to get Scarlett O'Hara out of her system. Then, in late August, Selznick wanted his Scarlett back again. The opening sequence bothered him. So for the third time Vivien Leigh and the

Composer, Max Steiner

Tarleton twins gathered on the porch of Tara and did it again, this time for Sam Wood. As she arrived on the set Selznick said to her, "My God, you look old!"

It was the same dialogue; only the costumes were different. Scarlett was now in virginal white. Wood had called for action and Scarlett again dismissed the

Tara becomes a refuge for members of the defeated army. From Frank Kennedy, Melanie learns that Ashley has been a prisoner of war which gives her hope that he might be alive. And Frank asks Scarlett if it is in order for him to propose marriage to her sister Suellen.

twins' talk of war. When they had first started shooting, all those months ago, no one gave the dialogue more than a moment's thought. It was simply the facile mind of a 16 year-old girl. Now the words assumed a new light and a new meaning for the next day Britain had declared war on Germany. *GWTW* was suddenly rather more than just a historical romance.

After the preview two things needed urgent attention. The music had to be written and the running time needed to be reduced by an hour. Oh, and that first scene still wasn't right. But just as Selznick was adding, finessing, vascillating, he was also taking away. Sequences were quickened by topping and tailing; minor scenes, such as the O'Haras' drive to the Twelve Oaks barbecue and Scarlett's wedding night, when she confined poor Charles Hamilton to a chair, were deleted. Little by little, frame by frame, the picture came down to just under four hours, still the longest film Hollywood had ever released.

It was time for another preview. On 18 October Hal Kern contacted the manager of the Arlington Theater in the pleasant resort of Santa Barbara, 100 miles up the coast from Los Angeles. He asked if Selznick International could preview *Intermezzo* but when the Selznick entourage arrived with forty-eight cans of film and sound the manager knew he would not be seeing *Intermezzo*. The triumph at Riverside was repeated.

Still Selznick was not satisfied. The cuts made between the first and

And then another weary soldier appears at the gates of Tara. Ashley Wilkes! Melanie runs to greet him and only Mammy restrains Scarlett from going as well. 'He's her husband, ain't he?'

second preview had produced some rather ragged transitions. In New York Ben Hecht had a day to write the captions that propel the story along. In Hollywood Selznick ordered ten days of retakes and found time to shoot additional material if he felt a sequence was not dramatic enough. One of these additional scenes—a remarkable one, when Scarlett, Melanie, the baby and Prissy hide under a bridge as Union soldiers thunder past above them—caused a final rift between Selznick and Victor Fleming. Earlier in the day Selznick had asked Fleming if he would object to a title card acknowledging the contributions of Cukor and Sam Wood. Fleming would certainly object and now he had to direct a scene in the pouring rain at a moment's notice. He had had enough of Selznick and *Gone With the Wind*. Fortunately, there wasn't any more left. It was all over, bar the music.

Max Steiner was one of Hollywood's leading composers. He was born in Vienna in 1888 and was an infant prodigy, graduating from the Imperial Academy of Music at the age of thirteen. He studied under Gustav Mahler, was a professional conductor by the age of 16 and emigrated to the United States in 1914, where he worked for the Broadway musical impresario Florenz Ziegfeld. His arrival in Hollywood inevitably coincided with the arrival of sound and, together with Erich Wolfgang Korngold, he pioneered the use of the richly thematic, symphonic movie score. Steiner had composed the music for several Selznick pictures, including *The Lost Squadron, What Price Hollywood?, King Kong, The*

Garden of Allah and *A Star Is Born*. He had also scored *Jezebel* and had researched the music of the American South and the Civil War period. Steiner was the ideal man for the job.

Hollywood composers have become accustomed to working *molto presto*. It is a constant irony that while producers and directors know only too well how a good score can transform an average picture into a great one, it is often their very last consideration, even an afterthought. Maurice Jarre, for example, had only six weeks to write, conduct and record the music for David Lean's *Doctor Zhivago* (1966) but within those six weeks he composed 'Lara's Theme', which became an international hit and a key element in the film's enormous popularity.

Steiner was hired in late August and was asked to write three hours of music in two months. He would then stay on at the Selznick studio for Hitchcock's *Rebecca*. At the same time, Steiner was completing work on *Four Daughters* at Warner Brothers, surviving the pace on a cocktail of thyroid extract and B-12 injections. When his work fell behind schedule, Selznick hired Franz Waxman and Herbert Stothart to spread the workload and vaguely threaten Steiner. This tactic produced the required result and Steiner completed his monumental work at the end of November. His great unifying theme, 'Tara', used over the main titles and at other key moments, would become one of the most familiar and best-loved pieces of movie music ever written.

From Sam, Scarlett learns that Wilkinson, an old adversary of the O'Haras, has joined forces with the carpetbaggers and has demanded $300 in taxes. She will ask Ashley for help. But Ashley is in no position to help, either financially or emotionally. He is consumed by defeat. 'You come to me for help and I've no help to give.' Scarlett seems to give in, both to hardship and her heart. 'Let's go away together, Ashley,' she says. 'There's nothing to keep us here.' 'Nothing?' Ashley replies. 'Nothing except honour.' They kiss each other hungrily and then agree to put aside their feelings for each other in order to rebuild the lives of their families and their land.

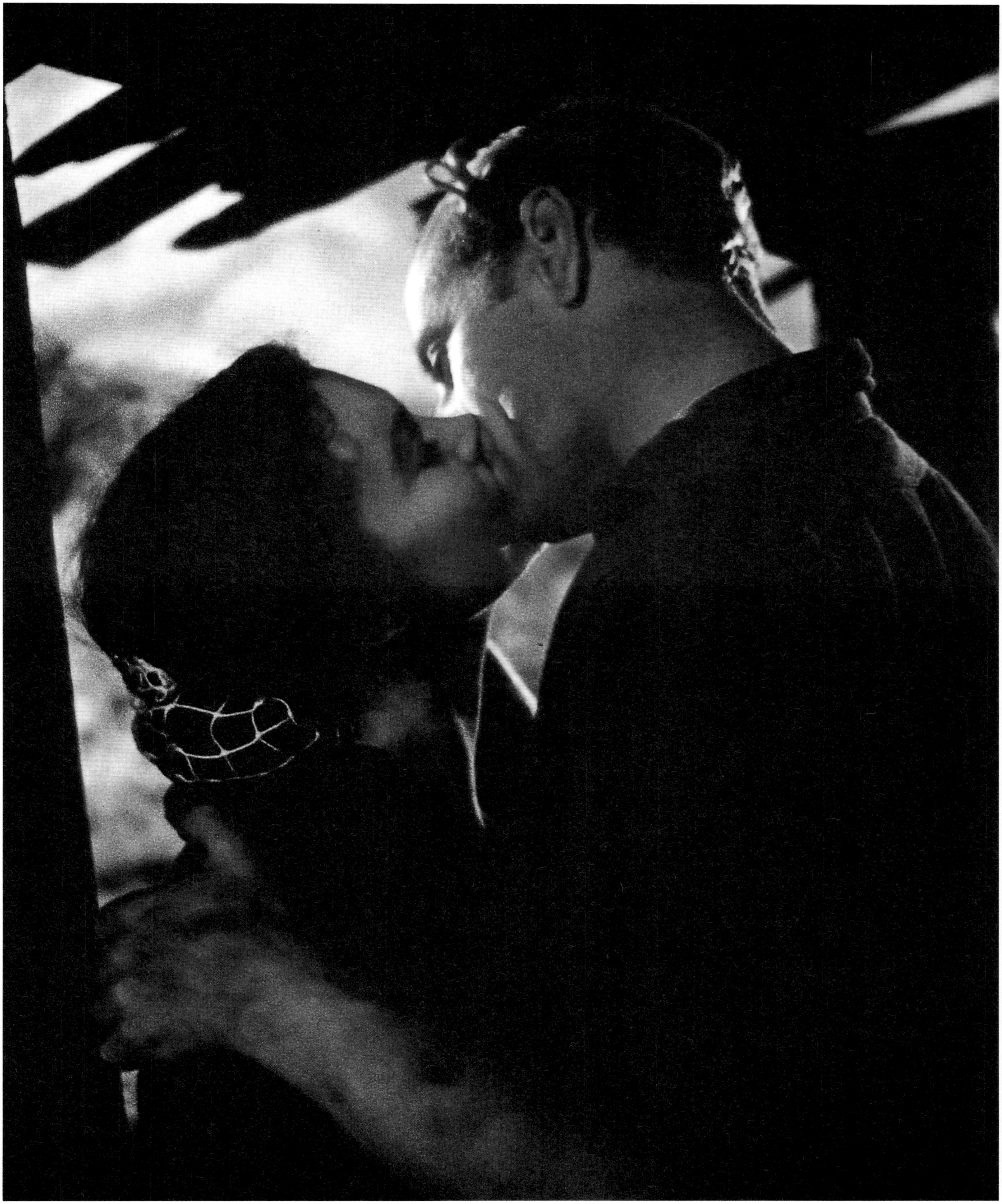

There remained one additional and extremely bothersome obstacle to overcome: moral turpitude. The guardian of Hollywood's and the nation's moral health was Will H. Hays, 'The Tsar of all the Rushes' as he was known. Hays, a former postmaster-general in President Harding's government, was appointed by the Hollywood moguls in 1922. At that time, the movie colony was portrayed in the press as drink-sodden, drug-ridden, sexually depraved, materially rich and morally bankrupt (so what else is new?). Several scandals, most notably the tragic case of Fatty Arbuckle who was charged with the manslaughter of a starlet in his hotel room, had made the pressure on the moguls unendurable. Two ideas were hatched to cultivate a decent and responsible image: an Academy of Motion Picture Arts and Sciences, which would award prizes and mediate in industrial disputes, and the Motion Picture Association of America, which would act as the industry's own censor and moral watchdog.

Hays was much liked in Hollywood and during the time of Prohibition he was an expert ambassador for Hollywood. He was not really a puritan, even though he introduced puritanism to Hollywood Babylon; he was simply a skilled politician. In 1933 he introduced the Hays Code, which dictated to producers what was and what was not acceptable on the screen in terms of visual and verbal material: cleavages were carefully measured and swear-words were forbidden. But Margaret Mitchell's novel ended with Rhett Butler drawing a short breath and

The loathsome Wilkinson arrives with his white trash lady friend and offers to buy Tara if Scarlett cannot pay the $300 in taxes.

saying lightly but softly, 'My dear, I don't give a damn.' Sidney Howard (or was it Ben Hecht or Selznick himself?), had embroidered this to, 'Frankly, my dear, I

A diversion from the London Blitz

don't give a damn.' This would not do. 'Damn' had not been heard on the screen since 1933. It was strictly taboo.

Selznick did not like the sound of 'Frankly, my dear, I just don't care,' even though he had actually got Fleming to shoot that version as 'insurance'. He knew also that the public would not like the sound of it either. On 20 October 1939 Selznick sent Hays a long and impeccably argued letter. 'As you probably know,' he wrote,

'the punch line of *Gone With the Wind*, the one bit of dialogue which forever establishes the future relationship between Scarlett and Rhett, is "Frankly, my dear, I don't give a damn". Naturally, I am most desirous of keeping this line and, to judge from the reactions of two preview audiences, this line is remembered, loved and looked forward to by millions who have read this new American classic.' Selznick went on to cite his previous work and its fidelity to the code. He quoted the *Oxford English Dictionary*, which defined 'damn' as nothing more than a vulgarism and hoped that the inclusion of the word in *GWTW* would be a useful precedent. Selznick's arguments won the day.

As *Gone With the Wind* finally went through the labs and the delicate process of colour grading, Selznick concentrated on MGM's plans to market and distribute the picture. There were disagreements and heated rows over performance times, venues, admission prices and advertising. Selznick wanted a top admission price of $1.65 per ticket, though eventually he settled for $1.50. Although MGM was generous to the public, they had driven a particularly hard bargain with exhibitors. Instead of the normal 30 per cent of box-office revenue, MGM would receive a massive 70 per cent.

Of course, MGM had a great deal of money invested in *Gone With the Wind*, but Selznick had more, and much else besides. It was his picture and everyone knew it. He wrote to Al Lichtman, a vice-president at MGM: 'This picture represents the

The hottest ticket in town

greatest work of my life, in the past and very likely in the future. I am associated with it in the public mind, and will be further associated with it. I do not intend, without every struggle that it is possible for me to put up, to be blamed for making a miserable botch of its exhibition.' Selznick never sent the letter; it

was merely his way of chairing a meeting without the annoyance of other people being present and his way of coming to terms with the fact that the film was in other people's hands now, and not entirely his own.

On 11 December 1939, three and a half years since Kay Brown wrote excitedly to Selznick, she now received a cable: 'Have just finished *Gone With the Wind*. God bless us one and all—DOS.'

It was 15 December 1939 in Atlanta, Georgia. By deciding to hold the world première of *Gone With the Wind* there Selznick had pulled off a tremendous publicity coup. He had missed by exactly one month the seventy-fifth anniversary of the burning of Atlanta.

The people of the city felt very possessive about *GWTW*. It was their picture and it was Margaret Mitchell's too. In 1939 Atlanta was a very modest state capital that still carried something of the glory, as well as the shame, of the Civil War. Georgians were proud of their heritage which *GWTW* reaffirmed for them.

Hollywood knew how to throw a movie première, though none was thrown quite so lavishly as the one in Atlanta. While Selznick had involved himself very closely with arrangements, inspecting the seating plans and requesting a personal link-up from his aisle seat to the projection booth, final responsibility lay with Howard Dietz, MGM's director of advertising and publicity. Dietz had persuaded

Scarlett insists he leaves immediately and the angry Wilkinson is chased away by the mentally deranged Mr O'Hara. But tragedy awaits: Mr O'Hara is thrown from his horse and he is later buried beside his wife.

the Governor of Georgia, E. D. Rivers, and the Mayor of Atlanta, William B. Hartsfield, to proclaim a three-day public holiday and had arranged for the façade of Loew's Grand Theater to be embellished with columns like an *ante-bellum* mansion. Dietz had turned the three Atlanta newspapers into branch offices of MGM's publicity department. There was the inevitable scrum for tickets to see the film and Hartsfield, forced to give up some of his allocation to the Governor, was placated by Dietz who promised that Clark Gable would escort the Mayor's daughter to the Junior League Ball.

The whole city turned out to welcome the delegation from Hollywood. MGM had chartered two aeroplanes which, to Selznick's annoyance, were emblazoned with '*MGM's Gone With the Wind*' along their fuselages. Clark Gable had decided to boycott the première in support of his friend Victor Fleming, who had no intention of going, but the star was eventually persuaded to attend by MGM's senior executives and he flew into Atlanta with Carole Lombard. In the other plane were the Selznicks, Vivien Leigh and Laurence Olivier, Olivia de Havilland and other cast members. There were speeches at the airport. David Selznick said, 'Ladies and gentlemen, we have entered Atlanta with humility and trepidation. We remain in gratitude. It is our fervent hope that this city of all cities will be pleased with our efforts.'

There was a motorcade to the theatre and the première was followed by

Scarlett is alone, but not defeated. She decides to ask Rhett Butler to give her the $300 and gets Mammy to make her a lavish dress from a green velvetine curtain. 'I've got to go looking like a queen.'

Rhett is a prisoner of the Yankees and is awaiting execution. He receives Scarlett in his cell and is excited by her beauty and her undiminished spirit. Scarlett's masquerade lasts until Rhett notices that her hands, once so delicate, now bear the callouses and scars of a field-hand. Angered by the sham and by her real lack of concern for his life, Rhett refuses to loan her the $300, even when she offers to sleep with him.

innumerable social functions. The next day, at a luncheon given by Governor Rivers, Kay Brown introduced David Selznick to Margaret Mitchell. Although Hattie McDaniel, the actress who played Mammy, was then in Atlanta, she did not attend the première—it was an all-white audience. At the end, after the applause, the cheers and the tears, Margaret Mitchell went on stage and spoke publicly for the first time. She said her handkerchief was wet and she paid tribute to Selznick's obstinacy and determination in assembling the perfect cast.

Just as he left his hotel for the theatre, Selznick had received a moving cable from Hollywood: 'I don't know whether to be wistful, noble or comic but I really send you all my love tonight—George Cukor.'

The press had seen *Gone With the Wind* in Hollywood on 12 December. A year before they had been calling it 'Selznick's folly'. Now they called it a masterpiece. The influential trade paper *Variety* thought that it 'was poised for grosses which may be second to none in the history of the business'. 'Is it the greatest picture ever made?' asked the critic of the *New York Times*. 'Probably not, although it is the greatest motion mural we have ever seen and the most ambitious film-making venture in Hollywood's spectacular history.' This critic concluded his review by summing up the feelings of the press: 'Anyway, "it" has arrived at last, and we cannot get over the shock of not being disappointed; we had almost been looking forward to that.'

As Scarlett leaves the jail empty-handed, Belle Watling arrives to offer Rhett some genuine comfort.

Overleaf: Atlanta rises from the rubble, if not the ignominy of defeat, and Frank Kennedy has become one of the city's leading merchants, having already cleared a $1000 profit. He will soon have enough capital to marry Suellen and settle down. Scarlett sees one last opportunity to save Tara, so tells Frank that Suellen has promised to marry someone else. She has him in her pocket, they marry and the future of Tara is assured. Suellen, of course, is furious at her sister's behaviour. 'It's all my fault,' says the forlorn Ashley. 'I should have committed highway robbery to get you that tax money.'

There were more parties, more chartered planes and more publicity stunts as *GWTW* opened at New York's Capitol and Astor Theaters on 19 December. On Christmas Day Selznick received a present of a gold watch from Jock Whitney his business partner. It was inscribed, 'David—Xmas 1939. Praise de Lawd. Jock.' And, finally, on 28 December, *GWTW* came back to Hollywood with a lavish première at the Cathay Circle. It played to capacity audiences in six major theatres over the Christmas and New Year holiday and then opened more widely in January.

On 29 February 1940 the Oscar ceremony took place in the Coconut Grove at the Ambassador Hotel. The out-going president of the Academy, the distinguished director Frank Capra, had persuaded his colleagues to allow a Warner Brothers crew into the room to film the proceedings which were also relayed to the nation on radio. Compared with the three-hour plus Oscar spectaculars today, the awards ceremony was then a modest affair with speechifying kept to a minimum.

At 11 p.m., after dinner, the ceremony began with Capra handing over the presidency to the producer Walter Wanger. The technical awards were distributed by the head of 20th Century-Fox, Darryl F. Zanuck, and then Wanger introduced the evening's host, 'The Rhett Butler of the airwaves, Bob Hope'. This was Hope's début as master of ceremonies, a position he was to hold for two decades. He walked on to the stage and quipped, 'What a wonderful thing, this benefit for

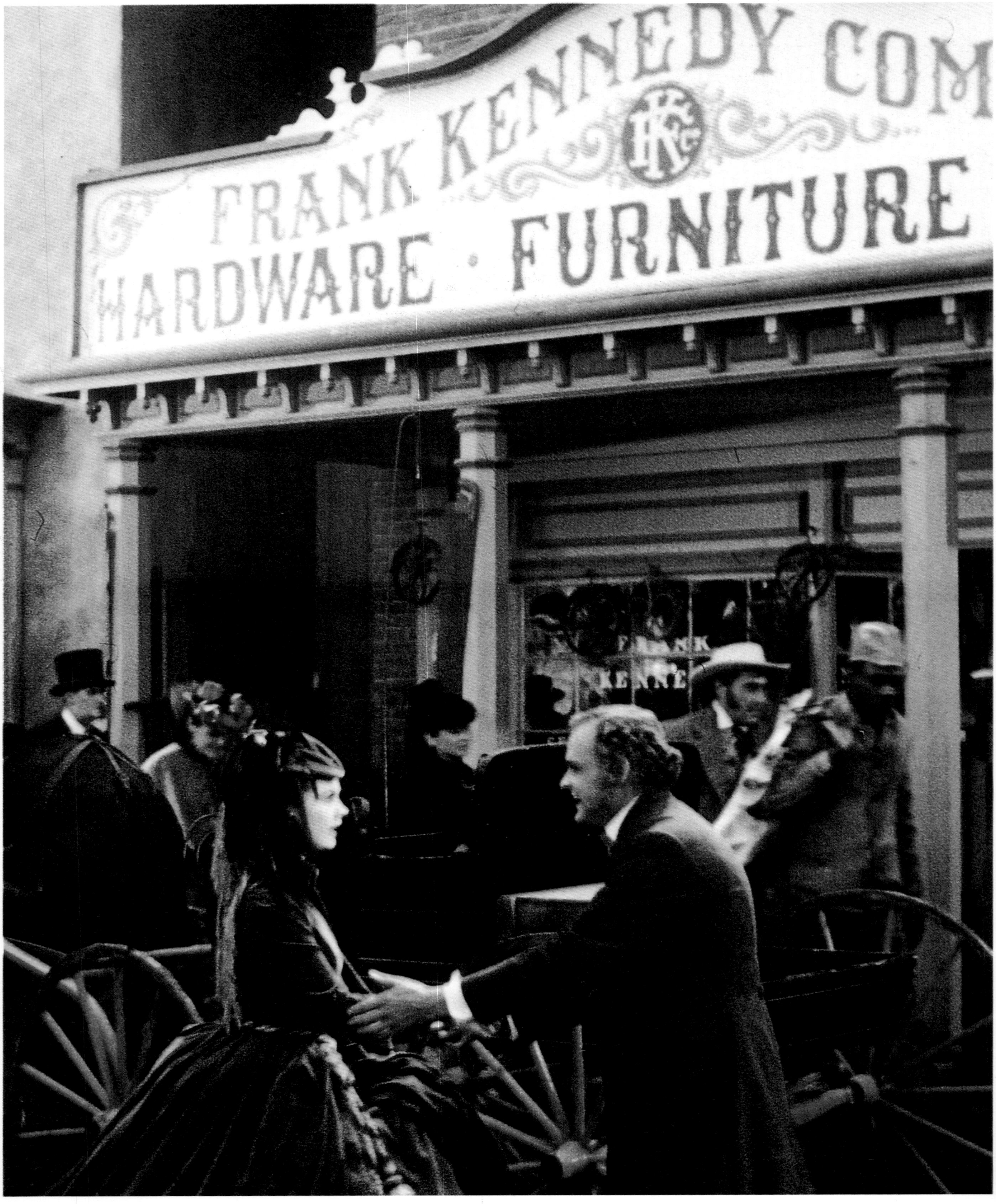
FRANK KENNEDY COM
HARDWARE · FURNITURE

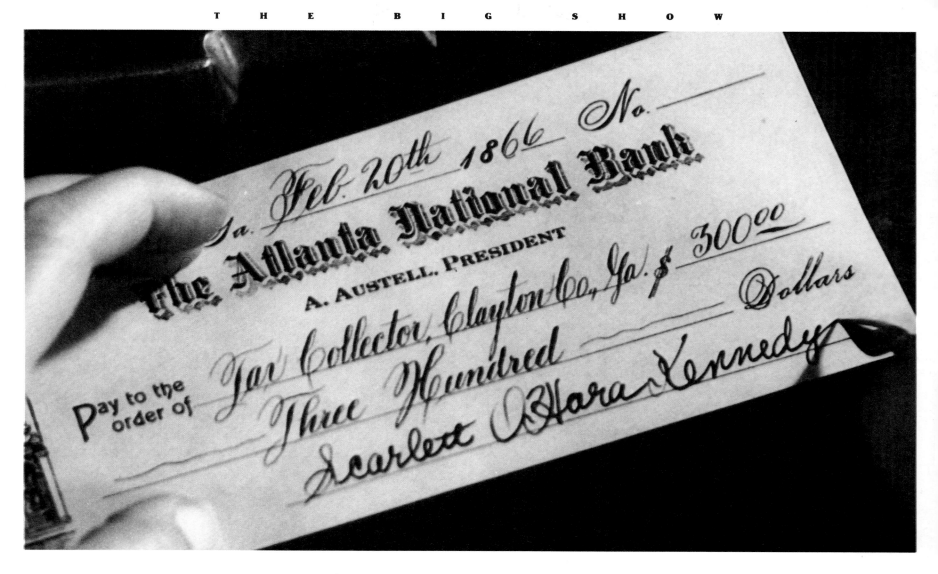

Overleaf: Scarlett hires convicts to work the mill since they are cheaper than 'darkies'. Frank is concerned that Scarlett seems to be taking over the business and showing no sympathy for those who owe them money.

'We are not a charitable institution,' she says. 'Great balls of fire! Don't bother me any more and don't call me sugar!' Scarlett is determined to beat the Yankees and the carpetbaggers at their own game and doesn't care what people think of her. The money rolls in.

David Selznick.' Everyone knew it was exactly that for the 8.45 p.m. edition of the *Los Angeles Times* had published the full list of winners. Thereafter, the results of the Oscars would remain secret until the envelope was opened.

Gone With the Wind had been nominated in twelve categories: Best Picture, Best Actor (Clark Gable), Best Actress (Vivien Leigh), Best Supporting Actress (Olivia de Havilland and Hattie McDaniel), Best Director (Victor Fleming), Best Screenplay (Sidney Howard), Best Colour Photography (Ernest Haller and Ray Rennahan), Best Interior Decoration (Lyle Wheeler), Best Sound Recording (Thomas T. Moulton), Best Original Music Score (Max Steiner), Best Editing (Hal C. Kern and James E. Newcom) and Best Special Effects (John R. Cosgrove, Fred Albin and Arthur Johns).

It won in all but four of these: Gable, much to his chagrin, lost out to Robert Donat in MGM's *Goodbye Mr Chips*; the sound recording award went to Universal's *When Tomorrow Comes* and the special effects award went to 20th Century-Fox's *The Rains Came*. For Gable it was really just bad luck, though the most surprising omission was the music award which went not to Max Steiner but to Herbert Stothart for *The Wizard of Oz*.

There was great emotion that night. Hattie McDaniel, trying to staunch a flood of tears, made an eloquent and dignified speech in which she pledged to be a credit to her race and to Hollywood. Olivia de Havilland, who was nominated in

the same category, rushed to congratulate McDaniel, burst into tears and had to escape into the kitchens to recover her composure. Vivien Leigh, accepting the award from Spencer Tracy, was a model of British aplomb. There was also a moment of sadness when author Sinclair Lewis announced that Sidney Howard had won the screenplay award. Howard had been killed in a tractor accident on his farm in September and became the first posthumous Oscar-winner.

There was great controversy that night as well. When Mervyn LeRoy announced Victor Fleming's name it was Selznick who accepted the award, saying that Fleming was ill. In fact, Fleming had boycotted the evening because of the enmity between him and Selznick. The next day Fleming would arrive at the Coconut Grove and accept his award for the benefit of the newsreel cameras. He thanked his crew but he did not thank Selznick.

Gone With the Wind had reaped eight Academy Awards, more than any previous film. But there were still two more awards to come. Selznick, in addition to winning an Oscar as producer to the Best Picture, was honoured with the Irving Thalberg Memorial Award. And William Cameron Menzies won a special award for 'Outstanding achievement in the use of colour for the enhancement of dramatic mood in the production of *Gone With the Wind*.'

For Selznick, the party was finally over. For him, for Vivien Leigh and the others who had lived in a world within a world, life could resume a more normal pattern.

Driving home alone through Shanty Town, Scarlett is attacked by a group of vagabonds. Later that night, Frank and Ashley decide to take their revenge on Scarlett's assailants. Rhett, who has bought his freedom, warns the waiting women that their men are riding straight into an ambush. He sets out to try and prevent a tragedy.

Rhett and Ashley return home drunk after an evening spent at Belle Watling's—or so it seems until the Union soldiers leave the house. Only then do Scarlett and Melanie realize that Ashley has been shot in the shoulder. As Scarlett tends Ashley, Rhett asks, 'Have you no interest in what's become of your husband, Mrs Kennedy?' Frank has been shot dead.

GWTW had become a financial blockbuster in the United States and now it was ready to conquer as much of the world as was possible in 1940.

On 18 April 1940 *GWTW* opened at the Empire Theatre in Leicester Square, London. When war broke out in September 1939 the British government closed all places of entertainment in the interests of public safety. However, this decision was very quickly reversed when it was realized how important entertainment, especially films, were to the nation's morale. So while the bombs of the Luftwaffe blitzed London, *GWTW* ran on and on and on. The Nazis had banned the film outright in all its occupied territories since they saw Scarlett as a figure of resistance and liberation. In Britain she was admired for these selfsame qualities. *GWTW* became a fixture, a touchstone, a symbol of survival and continuity. Selznick's epic offered an escape, a romantic dream and, in Scarlett's refusal to be beaten by war and by hunger, in her deep attachment to the land of her forefathers, and in her determination to win back the man she loved, Selznick offered a shattered world the hope that tomorrow is another day.

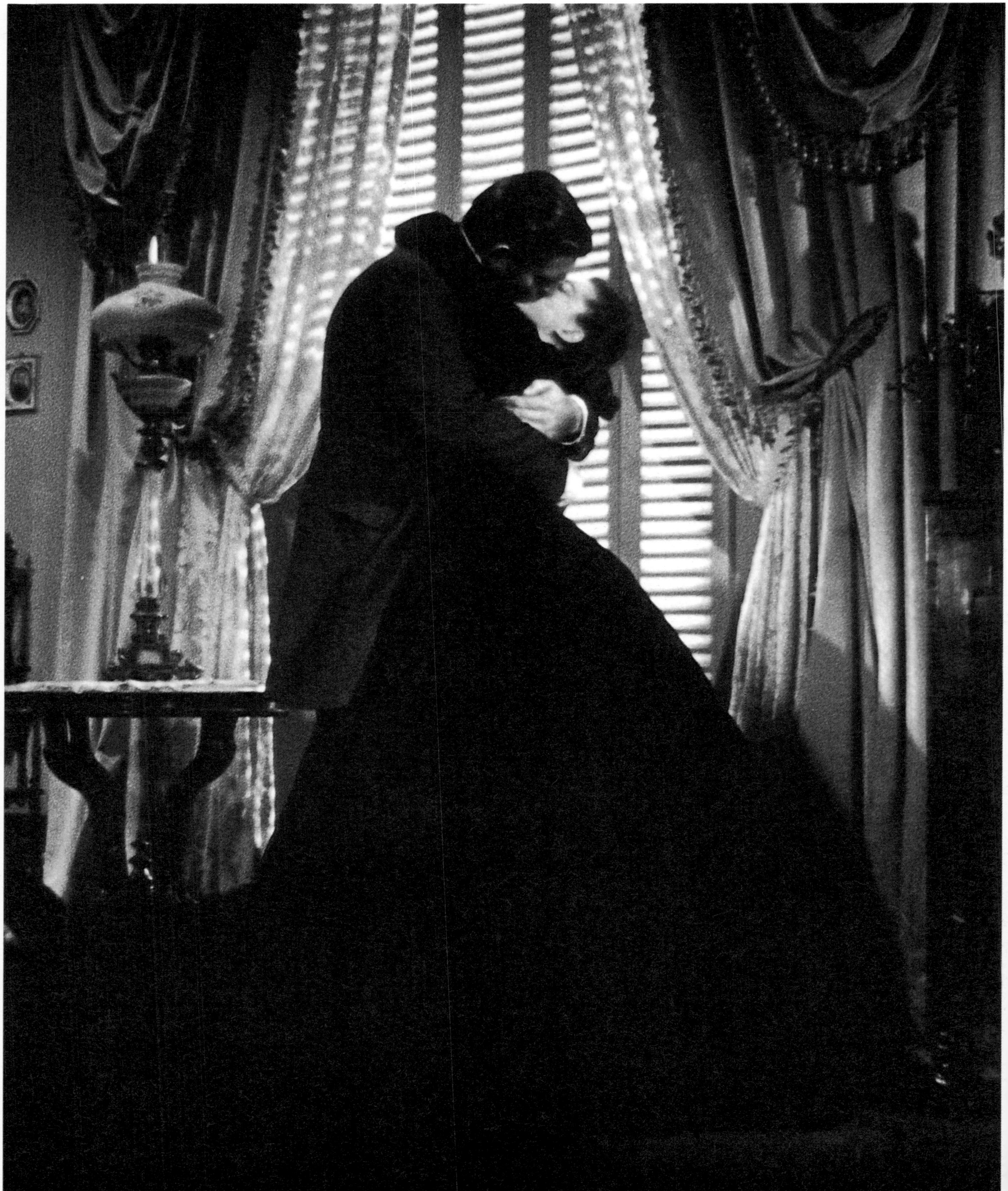

T H E   L E G E N D   O F

G O N E   W I T H   T H E   W I N D

It is in the nature and the chemistry of things that movies survive their stars and their producers and, sometimes, turn them into legends. The years may take their toll on the lustre and glamour of stars but their movies preserve them as they were, or as we thought they were, playing a role, speaking someone else's dialogue, made-up by experts, carefully lit and photographed, dressed in rented costumes, posing on pasteboard sets or against matte paintings. When we see *Gone With the Wind* today we know that most of the people on the screen and behind it are dead. It is a kind of mausoleum—not one of grey marble, echoing footsteps and hushed voices, but one of light and colour and the flare of youth. Yet even as we enjoy the picture and immerse ourselves in the Atlanta of Rhett Butler and Scarlett O'Hara there is a sadness as well for those shadows on the screen personify a kind of movie-making that is no longer with us. It was called Hollywood.

Gone With the Wind might have been completed in the autumn of 1939 but it lingered in the minds and in the hearts of some of those who made it. Of the principal contributors, only Leslie Howard remained untouched by it all. His aloofness on the set and his disdain for the character shows in his performance so that he seems distracted, his mind on greater things. No wonder Scarlett was in love with him for Ashley represents the romantic, the poet and the scholar, as much as the soldier or warrior. For Howard, the role was simply a means to an end. He produced *Intermezzo* and soon returned to England where his ambitions to direct were fulfilled; he directed, produced and starred in some powerful exercises in wartime propaganda. In 1943 he flew to Lisbon, on a secret mission for the British government it was said. He never returned. On the journey back to England the Germans, possibly believing that Winston Churchill was aboard, shot the plane out of the sky.

Clark Gable's career went into a gradual decline after *GWTW*. His marriage to Carole Lombard ended in tragedy in January 1942 when she was killed in an air crash while travelling across the US selling war bonds. Gable himself enlisted in the Air Force and went on bombing missions over Germany with an enthusiasm that some would describe as suicidal. He returned to Hollywood and MGM in 1945 and made *Adventure* with his old pal Victor Fleming. It was a failure and, like John Gilbert before him, Gable lost confidence and began drinking heavily. The spark, which had ignited the 1930s, had sputtered out. Gable's MGM contract expired in 1954 and was not renewed. He went freelance and the title of his first venture, *Soldier of Fortune* (1955), was as ironic as his last at Metro—*Betrayed* (1954). He demanded extravagant fees which were met because his name meant so much.

Dressed in mourning and feeling some genuine remorse, Scarlett receives Rhett at her house. 'I can't go on any longer without you,' he says. 'I've made up my mind. You're the only woman for me, Scarlett, since the first day I saw you at Twelve Oaks. Now that you've got your lumber-mill and Frank's money you won't come to me as you did to the jail. So I see I'll have to marry you. Would you be more convinced if I fell to my knees?' But Scarlett declines the offer. 'I don't like being married,' she says. 'Did you ever think of marrying just for fun?' asks Rhett. 'Marriage fun? Fiddle-de-dee.' But Rhett is persistent and pragmatic as ever. 'God help the man who really loves you.' Outwitted and outkissed, she relents and they honeymoon in New Orleans, later paying a nostalgic visit to Tara. Captain and Mrs Rhett Butler of Atlanta live in a new house of magnificent splendour and are attended by Mammy, Prissy and Sam. Before the year is out Rhett proudly holds his daughter, Bonnie Blue Butler.

He died of a heart attack in 1960 shortly after completing John Huston's *The Misfits* (1960) with Marilyn Monroe and Montgomery Clift.

Vivien Leigh's life was to be ravaged by mental and physical illness. Since she always preferred the theatre, she made only eight more films. After *GWTW* she returned to England to play Emma Hamilton to Olivier's Lord Nelson in *Lady Hamilton* (1941) and starred as Cleopatra in the box-office disaster *Caesar and Cleopatra* (1945). In fact, she became trapped in monumental historical roles (she was also Anna Karenina) until the director Elia Kazan recalled her to Hollywood for the film version of Tennessee Williams's *A Streetcar Named Desire* (1951). She had played the part on the London stage and would now win her second Oscar as the tragic Blanche DuBois. Leigh gave an extraordinary, passionate and moving performance as the declining Southern belle living on illusions and whose repressed sexuality is preyed upon by Marlon Brando's Stanley Kowalski. There were traces here of Scarlett O'Hara—her granddaughter, perhaps, fallen on hard times and unable to pull herself up—yet Leigh had finally exorcized that ghost of twenty years before. It was a great triumph, but tragedy was close at hand. In 1954, while filming *Elephant Walk*, she suffered a nervous breakdown, and her marriage to Olivier ended in divorce in 1960. She had been diagnosed as having tuberculosis in 1946 and suffered recurrent periods of illness associated with this until she finally succumbed in 1967. People who knew her found little irony in the

Scarlett decides not to have any more children—why, her waistline is no longer trim— which means denying Rhett his conjugal rights. As he receives this news he sees a portrait of Ashley has fallen from Scarlett's dressing table. Scarlett says her bedroom door will be locked in future. Overleaf: Rhett kicks the door open, goes downstairs and throws a whisky glass at Scarlett's portrait.

For the sake of their child, the Butlers' marriage will have the public veneer of love and devotion. But all of Rhett's love is directed towards Bonnie whom he teaches to ride.

fact that her final stage appearance was as the consumptive *Lady of the Camellias*.

Olivia de Havilland went from strength to strength and became the first important star to challenge the studio contract system. After *GWTW* she returned to Warner Brothers who continued to cast her in second-rate pictures. In 1944 she thought her seven-year contract had expired but Warners claimed an extra six months in view of the time she had spent on suspension. When she took the matter to court, Jack Warner managed to get her blacklisted by all the other studios. The court ruled in de Havilland's favour but Warner appealed, thus ensuring another period of unemployment for his rebellious actress, who set off to entertain the US troops in Alaska and the South Pacific. Eventually the Supreme Court rejected the appeal and de Havilland won not only her independence, but defeated the entire studio system. The blacklist was lifted and she enjoyed a string of hit movies until she married a Frenchman in 1955 and moved to Paris, where she lives now, occasionally appearing in TV mini-series when the mood takes her.

Victor Fleming's career, like Gable's, went into a tailspin after *GWTW*. He directed only five more films before his death in 1949. Sam Wood continued at a rate of knots, directing nothing especially distinguished, and served as president of the Motion Picture Alliance for the Preservation of American Ideals. He was one of Hollywood's most outspoken anti-communists and actively encouraged the McCarthy witchhunts which wrecked the careers of many actors, writers and

directors. Wood died in 1949. William Cameron Menzies died in 1957, after having been an uncredited director on Selznick's *Duel in the Sun* (1946) and the associate producer on *Around the World in 80 Days* (1956).

Getting fired from *GWTW* was a blessing in disguise for George Cukor. His subsequent work, with such eloquent and urbane performers as Cary Grant, Spencer Tracy and Katharine Hepburn, illustrates the glorious and civilized output of the often barbaric studio system. His final film, *Rich and Famous* (1981), was a rather lame attempt to recapture the glamour and the wit of his work in the 1930s and 1940s, although some amusement could be found in Candice Bergen's best-selling authoress from Atlanta who liked to whistle the theme music from *GWTW*. Cukor died in 1983.

And David O. Selznick? He had made the most famous and the most successful film in Hollywood's history. And the following year he won another Oscar as the producer of *Rebecca*. Selznick was never able to repeat that extraordinary two years of success and, inevitably, *GWTW* became something of a burden. He had peaked before his fortieth birthday. Selznick produced *Since You Went Away* (1944), *I'll Be Seeing You* (1944), Hitchcock's *Spellbound* (1945) and then launched into the florid western *Duel in the Sun* (1946) with his latest discovery, the actress Jennifer Jones. Selznick and Irene were divorced in 1949 and Selznick married Jennifer Jones the same year. He launched himself into

At the mill, Scarlett and Ashley comfort each other over their lost illusions. Their tender embrace, an expression of mutual sadness rather than desire, is observed by Mrs Meade and India Wilkes Naturally, they jump to the wrong conclusions and Rhett becomes convinced that Scarlett and Ashley are lovers. Overleaf: At Rhett's insistence, Scarlett attends Ashley's birthday celebrations—to the disbelief of the town gossips and to the delight of Melanie.

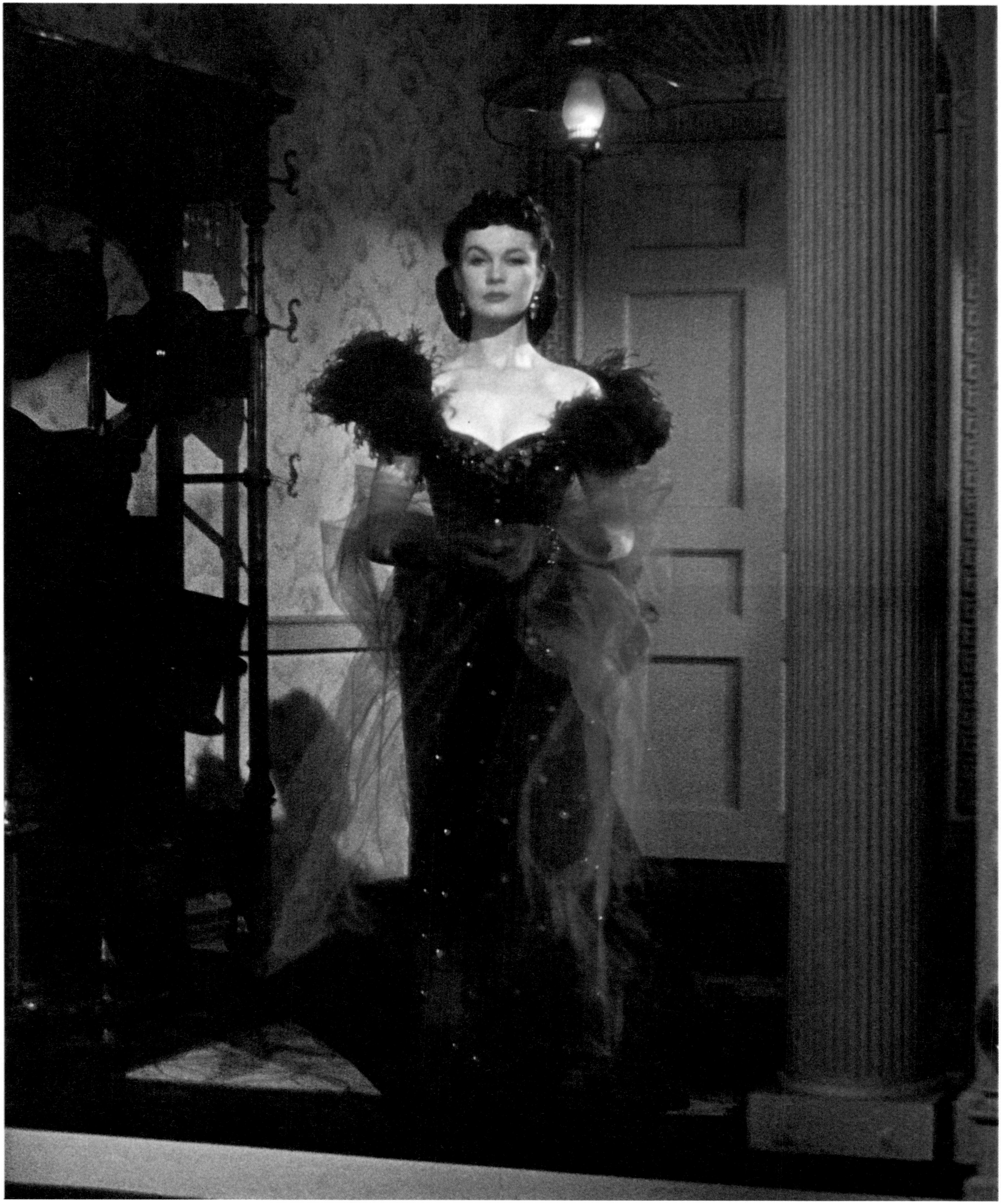

European co-productions, including *The Third Man* (1949) and another bizarre starring vehicle for his wife, *Gone to Earth* (1950), directed by Michael Powell and Emeric Pressburger. In Italy he joined forces with Vittorio de Sica for *Indiscretion of an American Wife* (1954), produced *Light's Diamond Jubilee* (1954) for television and made his final film, an adaptation of Ernest Hemingway's *A Farewell to Arms* in 1957. He always remained a brilliant and arrogant producer, a scourge of directors, but nothing he made equalled his great effort of 1939. His films began to cost too much and lose too much. Nevertheless, he was available to give advice to young film-makers like Dennis Hopper (who made home movies of the Selznick family), Alan Pakula and John Frankenheimer and even as he was assisting their careers he was observing the collapse of the studio system he helped create.

Gone With the Wind had cost $3,700,000 to make and a further $550,000 was spent on prints and advertising. Although not exactly unprecedented (the silent version of *Ben Hur*, made in 1925, had cost $4 million and barely broke even), it was still a reckless amount of money to spend on a single picture. Several industry analysts doubted the film could show a decent profit because few films managed to gross more than $1 million, let alone $4 million. But, of course, it did. Between 1932 and 1943 *GWTW* recorded rentals in the US of $31 million. In second place, with $8 million in rentals, was Walt Disney's *Snow White and the Seven Dwarfs*

Scarlett returns home to find a drunken Rhett wanting a divorce. By crushing her head between his hands he hopes to banish the dreams of Ashley from Scarlett's mind. Then he insists on claiming his conjugal rights, sweeping her up in his arms and taking her upstairs. The next morning Scarlett awakens as if from a blissful dream, but it does not last long. Rhett still wants a divorce and announces he is going immediately to London with Bonnie.

(1937), and in third place was MGM's *San Francisco* (1936) with $2.7 million. *GWTW* was not just a box-office smash—it was a phenomenon.

In 1987 *Variety* listed the all-time box-office champs and *Gone With the Wind* was ranked twenty-second with total rentals from the US and Canada estimated at $76,700,000. These figures are deceptive since the dollar of fifty years ago is not the dollar of today. In 1989 *Variety* calculated that *GWTW* has earned $840 million in today's dollars from its domestic and international screenings. This represents actual ticket sales in excess of $2 billion, making it undisputably the most profitable and most widely seen film in cinema history.

The irony is that this financial success eluded David Selznick. His initial profits from the first release have been estimated at $4 million after production, print and advertising costs had been deducted, and after MGM had taken the lion's share for distribution. This money was used immediately to write off outstanding loans and to finance future productions. At the same time, the massive amounts of money flowing in and out of Selznick's coffers made him liable for heavy income taxes. In order to reduce the burden of taxation it was decided to dissolve the company with Selznick and Whitney splitting everything.

In 1942 Selznick sold all his interests in *GWTW* to Jock Whitney for $400,000. The following year Whitney, whose interest in movies had waned, sold all his interests in *GWTW* to MGM for $2.4 million. Over the years—and there would be

In London Rhett comforts little Bonnie who suffers from nightmares and homesickness. Rhett and Bonnie return to Atlanta and Scarlett announces she is expecting a second child. Rhett is delighted by the news but Scarlett says, 'No woman would want the child of a cad like you.' 'Well, cheer up,' he says, 'maybe you'll have an accident.' The first of several tragedies then occurs: Scarlett goes to slap him, trips, and crashes down the stairs.

Scarlett has a miscarriage and Rhett cries his heart out to Melanie. He wants so much to make the marriage work and to have another child, but Scarlett's condition now makes that impossible. Melanie says that Rhett must not think that way. After all, she is to have another child, despite the dangers to her already frail health. 'Children are life renewing itself, Captain Butler.'

many dark ones ahead—*GWTW* would help keep MGM solvent. It became a kind of life insurance policy, to be redeemed at will or whenever one of the studio's big-budget pictures failed to make a profit.

MGM itself was in decline. In 1952 Mayer was deposed by Dore Schary and only the studio's musicals and the blockbusting *Ben Hur* (1959) saw them through the 1950s. Throughout the 1960s MGM was a pale shadow of its former self and in the 1970s it virtually withdrew from distribution and production. In order to generate some much-needed revenue, the studio diversified into the hotel business with the lavish MGM Grand in Las Vegas, which offered suites named after its most famous movies and stars. In order to raise capital the studio even auctioned its collection of props and costumes.

In 1967 MGM decided to re-issue *GWTW* in 70mm. The film was originally made with an aspect ratio of 1.33:1 and in 1954, to celebrate its twenty-fifth birthday, MGM had launched a major re-issue in the new widescreen ratio of 1.85:1 and stereophonic sound. In that version some of the original picture was inevitably lost, but the 70mm version was a travesty of the original and by that time the original colour, laboured over by Selznick, had become faded and fuzzy. But the publicity worked and audiences flocked to see it, though this hideously framed and blurred picture must have made them wonder what all the fuss had been about.

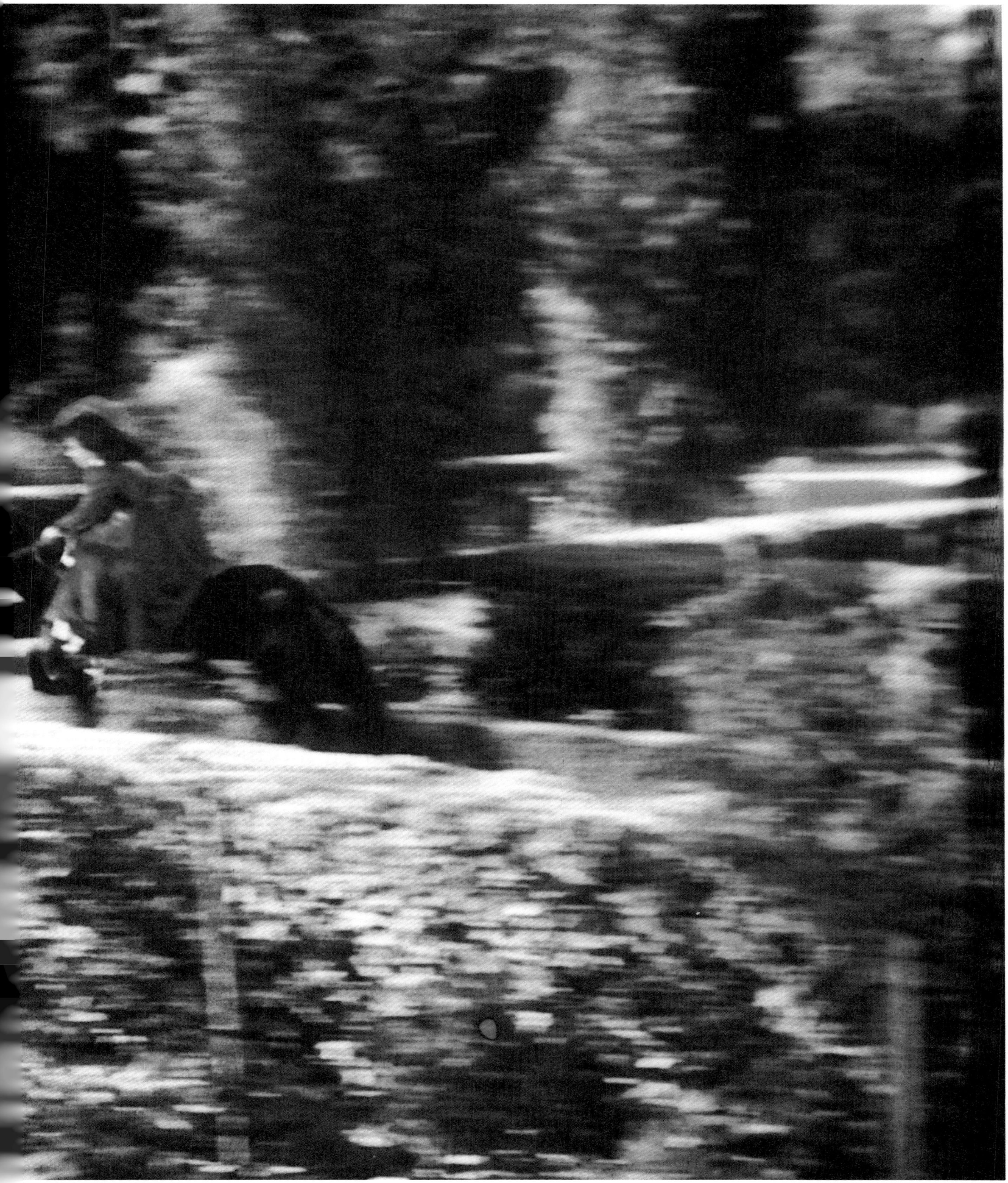

Then, in November 1976, MGM succumbed to the inevitable and sold *GWTW* to television. NBC paid $5 million for a single screening which was watched by a record audience of 110 million. The following year *GWTW* was sold to CBS for $35 million for twenty showings.

Throughout this period MGM had been bought and sold like an ageing race horse and in 1985 was owned by the Las Vegas millionaire Kirk Kerkorian. In an extremely complicated deal, MGM was sold outright to Ted Turner—of Atlanta, no less—for $1.5 billion. Turner was a cable television magnate who saw MGM and other studios not as places to make movies but as vast libraries of old movies which could be licensed to the proliferating cable TV stations. As soon as the ink was dry on the contract Turner sold back to Kerkorian the bits of MGM he had no use for.

Throughout the late 1980s Ted Turner was invoking the wrath of Hollywood film-makers for colourizing his library of Hollywood's old black and white classics. But in 1989, at a cost of some $250,000, Turner approved the careful restoration of *Gone With the Wind*, using the original colour matrices. The restored version opened in New York in February 1989 and for the first time in perhaps forty years audiences were able to see *Gone With the Wind* as Selznick intended it to be seen.

Since the 1970s there has been talk of a sequel, encouraged mainly by the rash

As Rhett and Scarlett restore their relationship, Bonnie is killed in a riding accident and Melanie becomes fatally ill. Overleaf: With her dying breath, Melanie asks Scarlett to look after Ashley and to be kind to Captain Butler: 'He loves you so.' Ashley and Rhett await Melanie's passing. Scarlett embraces Ashley and Rhett walks out in high dudgeon. For the first time in her life, she realizes the depth of Ashley's love for Melanie and that the only man who loves her is Rhett. She turns to him, but he is gone.

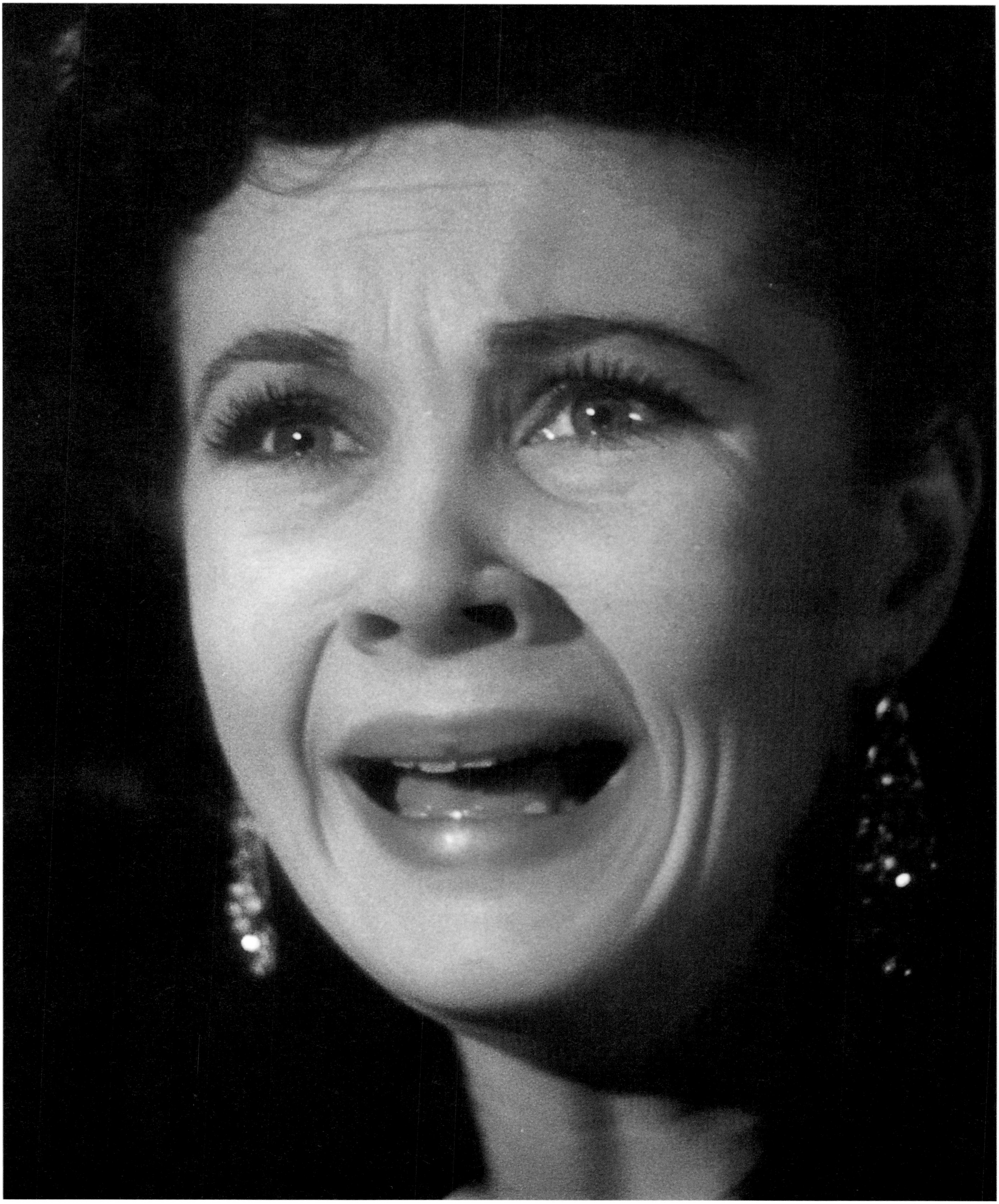

of successful sequels such as *The Godfather Part II* (1974) and *French Connection II* (1975). Nothing came of it because of the expense, because no one could figure out what happened next and because MGM's management was constantly changing. But the publishing world is slightly more stable and in 1987 Margaret Mitchell's publishers, Macmillan, announced that after years of searching for the right author, Alexandra Ripley had been commissioned to write *Gone With the Wind II* which is due for publication in 1990.

A sequel to the movie now seems inevitable, even if the prospect of knowing whether or not Scarlett managed to get Rhett back is hardly a thrilling one. Part of the enduring appeal of the picture is its concluding mystery. We take it home with us and privately ponder the later lives of the characters. If a story is stretched beyond its natural limits it turns into soap like *Dallas* or *Dynasty*. But whether the sequel is a movie or a TV mini-series, there will doubtless be a frantic search for Rhett Butler and Scarlett O'Hara and a lot of ballyhoo. Except there are no Gables now, no Vivien Leighs, no system, no glamour and, most significant of all, no Selznicks.

Back in 1939 Lee Rogers, the film critic of the *Atlanta Constitution*, wrote 'Gone With the Wind opens a new film era. It has everything a great picture could have. It has everything that everybody ever wanted.' With hindsight we can see that Rogers

Scarlett runs back to Rhett and tells him that Melanie has died. 'She was the only completely kind person I ever knew,' he says. Scarlett says that Melanie's last wish was that she should look after Ashley and Rhett. But Rhett is filled with bitterness: 'It's convenient to have the first wife's permission, isn't it? Now your dreams of Ashley can come true.' Crying uncontrollably, Scarlett says, 'I love you.' 'That's your misfortune,' says Rhett as he closes his suitcase and walks to the door.

At the door Scarlett makes one last attempt to make Rhett stay. 'Rhett! Where shall I go? What shall I do?'
Overleaf: Rhett says, 'Frankly my dear, I don't give a damn,' and walks out of Scarlett's life and into the mists of Atlanta.

was wrong. But in the heat of the moment of Atlanta, choked by Selznick and MGM's ballyhoo, that kind of confusion is understandable. In fact, *GWTW* marked not the beginning of a new era but the end of an old one.

Ahead were the dark days of the war, the McCarthy blacklist and the demise of the moguls and the dream factories they created. It is true that after *GWTW* some great movies lay ahead, and only two years later there came a film that did herald a new era—Orson Welles's *Citizen Kane* (1941), which was made at RKO for $800,000 and allowed its director complete control. Actually, many of the special effects in *GWTW*—one thinks particularly of the mattes, the false ceilings and some of Garmes's lighting effects—were used extensively in *Kane*. But Welles's film was aesthetically innovational and politically and historically sophisticated where *GWTW* was traditional and blinkered. *Kane* gave audiences something to chew on, it made them work, they had to sift some of the ingredients, draw allusions and come to conclusions whereas *GWTW* served up everything on a plate and you just tucked in.

If one evaluates movies in terms of their influence, then *GWTW* is virtually worthless. The sheer scale and expense of the picture prohibited imitations and perhaps only Selznick's *Duel in the Sun* and the equally overwrought Southern melodramas—MGM's *Raintree County* (1957) and *Home From the Hill* (1960)— are seriously indebted to it. And in the cascading drama of Part Two, when

characters drop like flies and when each scene ends on an emotional cliffhanger, we see the seeds of TV soap-operas such as *Dallas* and *Dynasty*.

At the same time, the enduring popularity of *GWTW* owes relatively little to the casting. Unlike Humphrey Bogart in the Forties or James Dean and Marlon Brando in the Fifties, Clark Gable, a creature of the Thirties, has not become the centre of a cult, an icon of rebellion and healthy cynicism. And Vivien Leigh does not possess the mystique that attends Garbo, Bette Davis, Ingrid Bergman or Marilyn Monroe. Victor Fleming is forgotten and producers, even great ones like Selznick, are always out of fashion.

GWTW was old-fashioned on the day of its release and remains so. It simply gave audiences more of what they were already accustomed to seeing. Its popularity and its own myth is its best defence. It doesn't really matter that Part One is superbly paced and structured or that Part Two manages to be rushed and overlong at the same time. Even the film's patronizing—if not racist—portrayal of the blacks is submerged in its mythologizing of America. The film contains some fundamental yearnings—for the agrarian past, for chivalry and heroism. Its hero turns from cynicism to commitment (much like the heroes played by Bogart in the years ahead) and then to cynicism. Its heroine might be the victim of sexist dialogue and even marital rape but she is a survivor, a true American who, in one way or another, speaks for us all.

Scarlett: 'I can't let him go, I can't. There must be some way to bring him back … Oh, I can't think about this now, I'll go crazy if I do. I'll think about it tomorrow.' She slumps on the staircase and voices, words and memories fill her head— her father, Ashley, 'land is the only thing that matters …something you love better than me …the red earth of Tara …something worth dying for, Tara, Tara, Tara!'

The voices clear and Scarlett's way forward is also clear. 'Tara. Home. I'll go home and I'll think of some way to get him back. After all, tomorrow is another day.'

Selznick was a man of his time. There would be other obsessive geniuses but few with his flamboyance or his arrogance. And those that might be compared to him are mainly directors, not producers. How Selznick must have worried over the rise of the director! In common with the other movie moguls—the Mayers, the Cohns, the Zanucks and the Goldwyns—Selznick could not move with the times. He had given Hollywood and America an anthem and some kind of masterpiece—of logistics, of filmed literature, of popular romance. If he could not rise above that peak it was because it was no longer necessary. The world had moved on, and so had the movies. After all, *GWTW* would always exist and so would the audience. It was and remains the pinnacle of what we mean by Hollywood. Look for it only in books for it is no more than a dream remembered. It was a civilization of sorts, a civilization gone with the wind.

THE

A SELZNICK INTE

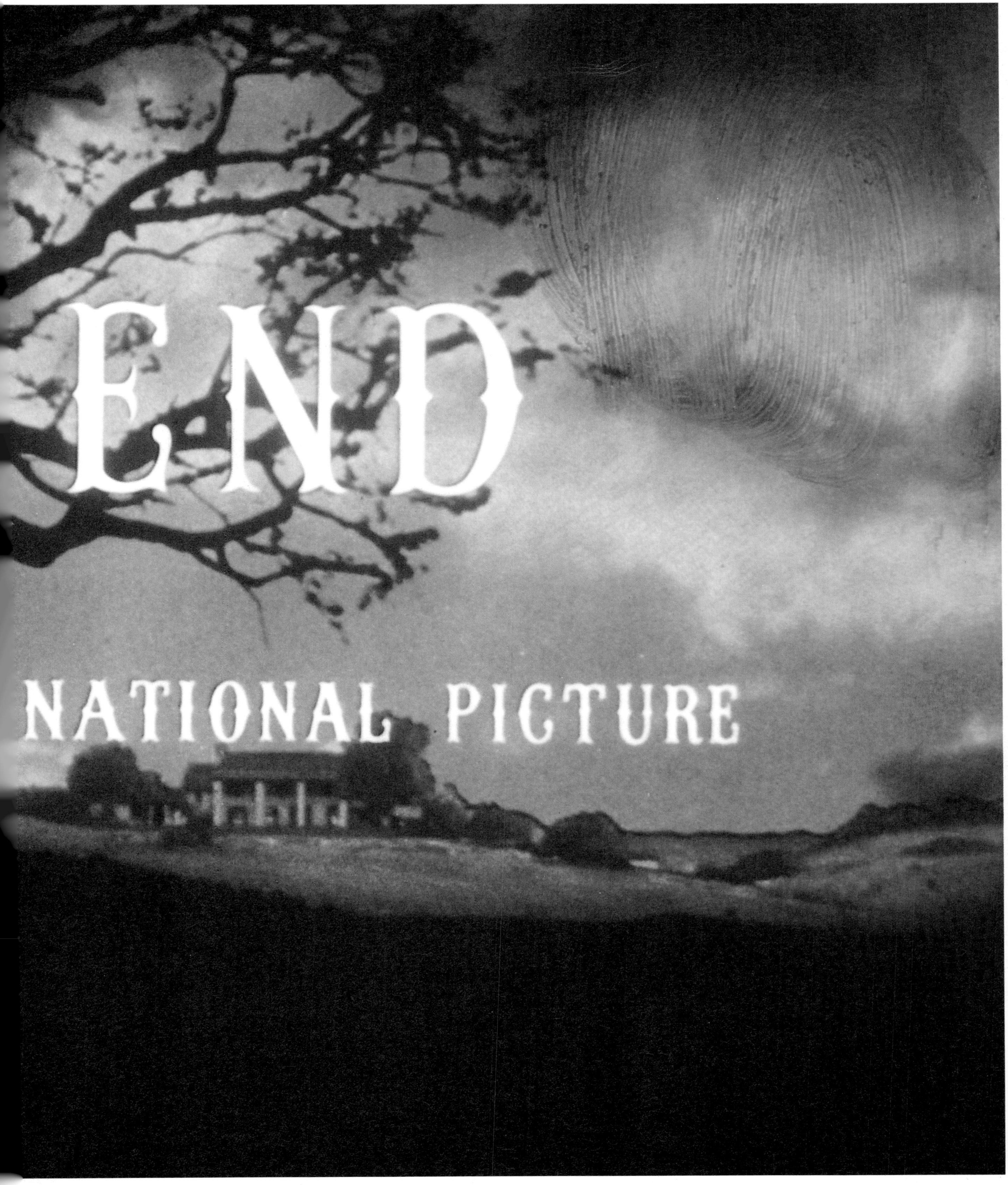
END
NATIONAL PICTURE